The Mule Companion

A Guide to Understanding the Mule

by

Cynthia Attar

CCB Publishing
British Columbia, Canada

THANK YOU

A heartfelt thank you goes out to all those willing mule enthusiasts who submitted personal photos to this fourth edition.

Your love for your mules shines through loud and clear— which is the fundamental message of this entire book.

First Edition: April 1993
Second Edition: May 1996
Third Edition: November 1998
Fourth Edition: December 2009
Library of Congress Catalog Card Number 93-92659
ISBN 13: 978-0-9651776-5-8
ISBN 10: 0-9651776-5-3
Composed and Printed in the United States of America

Publisher: CCB Publishing
             British Columbia, Canada
             www.ccbpublishing.com

COVER PHOTO STORY

Cover photo: Chuck Showers and Kate, Bakersville, NC.

I felt drawn to share the story of Chuck and Kate, as it depicts the bond between person and mule—the true reason we dearly love our long eared equine friends. This story was written by Chuck's wife, Carole Showers. The level of bond between the two is clearly displayed in this photo, Chuck and Kate in Chapter 14, and so many photos between the pages of this book.

Chuck grew up always wanting a mule. Kate was very young when we got her (about 4 years old). Subtle and not so subtle signs told us that she had not been started well at all, as she had 'cherries' on the sides of her mouth where someone had sawed a horrible bit back and forth. After we got her home we could also tell that she had probably been tied up and whipped, because if you tied her off to groom her, and then walked up towards her back end, she would hunker down in fear and try to fold herself in two. In the early days, she would start getting uncomfortable when you asked her to do something. Soon she would just blow up and go into self-preservation—nothing vicious towards us, just an "I've got to get out of here and protect myself" mode.

Don't get me wrong, a lot of times Kate caused—and still causes—her own problems. She is quite a thinker (more so than most mules I've met) and it can certainly be like dealing with a toddler. But the flip side, is that she is one of the most 'in your pocket' mules I've ever seen. Chuck has had her now for several years. Kate has really come to trust Chuck. She will now stop the "theatrics", listen to him, and calm herself down. She has also taught Chuck how to collect himself and think a few steps ahead of her. They have really grown together!

We get a lot of ribbing from people that just can't understand why the heck we would want to ride mules! Chuck even had to convince me! I started out riding a horse, but after a year ended up getting Tess, my current mule. Now that I have Tess, and Chuck has Kate, we wouldn't trade them for the world!

TABLE OF CONTENTS

INTRODUCTION

"Mules? You train mules? Why mules?" People have asked me this for many years. The question is familiar, yet I still don't have a satisfactory answer for those who have yet to see the immense value of a mule-human partnership. My favorite response is, "Well, it's a nasty job, but someone's gotta do it!" Sometimes folks will take me seriously and respond with, "Oh, yeah, I guess it is."

I've had a fascination with mules for quite some time. Before I tell you *my* story on mules, let me assist you in getting the most out of this book. When I originally compiled the research, my goal was to gather all the bits and pieces of information and to sort them out to portray an accurate picture of this valued worker and partner, sort of a mule owner's manual. I did not intend to get into a how-to book, as that only limits you to doing what I say. I'd rather enable you to take all the information presented and make decisions for yourself—*this* is the definition of wisdom. Hopefully, this book will spur you to be a better mule trainer than I ever was or will be.

The Mule Companion is divided into three sections: Beginning, Intermediate, and Advanced. This is so the meat of the book will not get lost, whether it is picked up by an accomplished mule trainer who thinks the book is only on the history of mules, therefore jumping to the conclusion that it is too elementary for his or her expansive mule knowledge, or by a newcomer to mules, who immediately gets discouraged at the vast, in-depth psychology of mules. Regardless of your mule wisdom level, this book has something for everyone, including bits of humor.

The first section is dedicated to an introduction of the mule. If you are new to mules, start at the Beginning section. This section will give you an all around view of the mule. The Intermediate section talks of things every mule owner should know. If you already know most all this information, be assured that you will still learn something about your hybrid when you delve into the Advanced section. This third section will provide you with mule wisdom, things to ponder, philosophy to consider, and facts and perspectives on why those long-eared critters do what they do. This section is to help you expand your awareness and to bring mules and humans closer together in their understanding of each other, so neither needs to be hurt when working together.

As a mule trainer and not a writer, I put forth much effort to accomplish the goal of writing a mule owner's manual. When the previous editions were published, it was the best I could do with the writing and publishing skills I had at the time. Finally, through much trial, many errors, unwavering determination, and progressing skills, this fourth edition is the final book, that which I envisioned years ago.

I must explain that I have no gender prejudice, but for simplicity I have referred to all mules and handlers as "he." All trainers, owners, riders, and anyone else who handles a mule has been designated as "handler" throughout this book. Please take no offense to this gender terminology, as the message is still the same.

I have heard many mule stories—I am a good listener, ya know! I have found some to be delightfully humorous, some tragically disastrous, and some a little of both. All the stories are precious gems to hear—and to behold. I enjoy watching the storyteller fondly recalling incidents regarding his or her beloved mules. Rarely have I had an opportunity to tell my own mule story! But since you asked…here is how I got hooked on mules.

A few years back I became reacquainted with an old-time family friend. As a current horse trainer, I had a strong desire towards driving and harness work, which led me right into draft horses and mules. Kenny just happened to indulge in a hobby of breeding draft horses that produced the cutest long-eared foals I had ever seen! All that I knew about mules at that time was their reputation for being great working animals. Those darling little foals of Kenny's, with their long ears, long legs, and unusually independent minds, really captivated my interest.

Author, Cynthia Attar, and best friend, Sally the Wonder Mule.

Photo courtesy of Michelle Dirkse, Seattle, WA.

There was one incident that hooked me forever on mules. One spring I decided to move one of Kenny's Belgian mares and her young mule colt to an adjoining pasture that was full of lush grass. All cross-fences within the twenty acres were made of electrified wire. I unhooked and opened the electric gate which separated the sparse field they were in from the lush field next door. With mom in hand, anxious to feast on the meal ahead, we smartly danced through the wide gate, expecting the mule colt to follow closely behind as a horse colt would. This young mule colt did as expected until he got to the opened gate, and then suddenly screeched to a stop. The field was quite large, so I kept leading the Belgian mare further and further away from the opened gate and her braying son, hoping the young mule's desire to be with his mom would overshadow whatever seemed to be the problem in exiting through that gate. Finally, the mare and I reached a tree in the back field. Mom quickly forgot about the lush grass and her lunch excitement turned to nervousness in being separated from her son. I was sure that the youngster would finally decide to follow mom and join us in the new field, but no way! This innocent young john mule was definitely not willing to leave his sparse field for any reason!

Now, most folks would say, "What a dumb animal." Instead, I said, "Wow, I wonder why he didn't follow along as a horse colt would. This mule obviously has his own set of logical reasons that I don't understand. I wonder what's going on in that brain of his and how I can get him to change fields." This simple spring event began my rewarding—yet frustrating—challenge of working with mules.

I'm not going leave you hanging. I'm sure you're asking, "Whatever happened to that mule colt? Did he ever get through the gate?" Well, as all you smart mule folks know by now, evidently the john mule had gotten shocked by the electric fence gate in his first few months of life and there was no way anyone, for any reason, was going to make him walk through that gate with the possibility of getting shocked again! As it turned out, I finally turned the dancing mom around and returned her to her son in the sparse field. We exited through a separate wooden gate with the foal bounding along happily and closely. We then passed through an unfamiliar electric fence gate to arrive at the new pasture. Ah, success at last!

After that, my compelling quest to understand the mule's mind began by searching through books (we didn't have the Internet at that time, but merely libraries and bookstores). All I could find were horse books, and only a few of them had any information about mules. Knowledgeable local mule folks were hard to come by. My mule education continued by purposefully deciding to take on some mules to train, to learn just what it took to get the same results from mules as from horses. I found that some of these longears' reactions were mind-boggling. Just when I expected them to do a certain thing, they would outsmart me and do another. I knew I had to be on my toes in working with them because they seemed to know much more about me than I did! Wow, what an intriguing challenge! Luckily, my horse instincts, intuition, and strong desire for a challenge (essential ingredients when training mules) helped me to produce trained mules that were "okay" in those days. It wasn't until I expanded my horse and mule training education by learning from the best starting/breaking trainers in the country that I was able to produce a top quality, *willful* partner. Training horses then became "ho-hum," but training mules became exciting and challenging.

A Note of Appreciation

I would like to express my great appreciation to Tom Dorrance, Ray Hunt, John and Josh Lyons, Pat Parelli, Monty Roberts, and many others who are skilled in equine psychology, for allowing us to view their gentle, yet amazingly effective styles of training. I also would like to express my immense gratitude to a variety of animal communication specialists who have developed the ability to communicate with animals on a telepathic level, which has opened my eyes as to what is really going on in the thoughts of our friends.

A thank you to Lydia Hiby for "reading" Sally the Wonder Mule's mind to find her whereabouts when she decided to explore the countryside for two weeks by herself. Thanks also to Penelope Smith, Georgina Cyr, and so many others for giving classes on teaching us laypeople to further develop our own psychic ability with animals. Thanks also to J. Allen Boone, Michael Roads, and Linda Tellington-Jones—just to name a few—for the wondrous books that are educating the public on this awakened awareness. (See Suggested Reading.)

The following is what mules would like to say to horse owners who have expanded outwards and are working with mules:

We are a different animal than horses. Our method of getting through to you may not be like a horse does. Study your mule and figure out what s/he is trying to tell you. If you expect us to act as horses, you will not understand us as well. Each mule will do what it takes to be heard. The more the human tries to determine what the mule is saying, the less obnoxious the mule needs to be to get through to the human. Having only the horse for a point of reference, some humans will quit listening when the mule exhibits a behavior that is not horse-like.

If the mule were to share his view of the human race, and how he fits in as a partner, he would most likely say:

We mules see you [people] as a struggling race with many problems to overcome. We are here to keep you balanced. By that we mean when you are struggling so, you are out of balance with peace. If you watch us mules, we are usually happy. You too can be happy if you model yourselves after us. That is not to say that there can be no room for individuality; as you know, each mule is a unique individual on his/her own.

When you are struggling more than is needed, we mirror your discomfort. Whenever you find that you have a problem with us, it is because you are in disharmony with yourself. This goes for other animals as well, but you will find that mules will be at peace when you are at peace and in disharmony when you are in disharmony. Our goal is to be at peace with you and try to get you to be at peace with us.

These long-eared creatures are a complicated animal, and some folks may decide that having a mule is simply too much mind-work and frustration. My personal experience in training mules and raising Sally, my beloved molly mule, is far too rewarding to put into mere words.

With the massive universal changes happening in this day and age, it is not unforeseen that we all may be given the opportunity to use mules as our beloved beast of burden again. If we end up living off the land, without today's modern conveniences, we just may be glad we have prepared our mules and ourselves by understanding, appreciating, and training properly!

Enjoy~

Cynthia Attar

BEGINNING SECTION

INTRODUCING THE MULE

CHAPTER 1:
MULES OF THE *PAST*

MULES HELPED TO BUILD AMERICA

Mules have made tremendous partners with both men and women in years past. These hard-working, dedicated, long eared equines have quietly labored side by side with man to build this great country of America, while man has taken virtually all the credit! It's time we give credit where credit is due. Today we handsomely salute the mule in honor and appreciation of tasks well done. What are those tasks in which the mule has participated with man in the past? Sit back while we travel through time on a quick, yet fascinating journey of yesteryear, viewing the amazing mule in teamwork with man.

Ancient Mule

Through research, zoologists theorize that mules were first bred some thirty centuries ago. Anacreon (572–488 BC) was a Greek lyric poet who credited the Mysians (people from Mysia, an ancient country in northwestern Asia Minor) with being the first to breed mules.[1] It seems as though way back in ancient Israel and Homeric Greece man solicited the aid of the mule. These small, dedicated mules willingly performed the none-too-exciting task of treading an endless circle, turning wheels to generate power used by man.

Even explorer Christopher Columbus knew the value of mules. In 1493, on his second sea voyage to the New World of America, Columbus decided to ship mules to this new continent to be used as man's beast of burden. These small mules—compared to what you see today—were said to be of indifferent quality and were little more than curiosities. Yet they significantly increased the reputation of the mule to be that of a great working animal. It is said that the first pioneers who cut paths across North America rode mules—rather than horses—in the mountains and over deserts, in areas where food and water were scant. Mules remained at this smaller size and limited ability until the era of George Washington.

George Washington's Dream

Prior to the turn of the eighteenth century, George Washington was a prominent American farmer who recognized the invaluable qualities of the mule. Washington's eighteenth-century dream was to take the current mediocre mule stock and develop it into what he called *an excellent race of mules*. Washington desired to increase their size, strength, style, and working ability—therefore greatly increasing the rate of crop production—to further develop the mule's skills, ability, and reputation as man's favorite beast of burden.

As you probably know (and we will delve further into this in later chapters), a mule is a cross between a mare horse and a jack donkey. There were plenty of fine horses in America during this era; however, the American donkeys were small and inferior. During the late 1700s, Spain began proudly breeding the finest donkey stock in the world. These jacks were large, thick-boned, and had good attitudes. Washington developed a burning desire to bring these larger Spanish jacks to America to breed with top-quality light and draft horses in order to fulfill his lifelong dream of developing the

Illustration courtesy of Public Domain

October 26, 1785, is the day George Washington began developing the size and strength of mules you see in America today.

mule. There was only one problem that stood in the way of Washington realizing his dream, however. The Spanish loved their long-eared friends and guarded their prized donkey stock jealously, forbidding the exportation of both jacks and jennets (male and female donkeys, respectively). To Washington, this one major problem seemed to be insurmountable under the circumstances. Somehow, there had to be a way to overcome this hurdle so these fine donkeys could be brought to America to be bred with high-quality horse mares.

Word of Washington's intent and desire to create *an excellent race of mules* soon reached the King of Spain. King Charles III surmised that with George Washington becoming a foremost citizen in a brand new nation, there might be numerous benefits in obtaining a positive affiliation with this prominent farmer. In what seemed to be a miracle to Washington, King Charles III purposely caused an exceptional Andalusian jack and jennet to arrive in Mount Vernon, Virginia, on October 26, 1785! Washington's dream was fulfilled! Now he could finally begin breeding his best mares to fine, larger jacks.

The sizable young jack that was shipped in from King Charles III of Spain appropriately became known as "Royal Gift." In the course of the first year in his new home, Royal Gift disappointingly presented himself as a shy, reserved breeder. Nevertheless, he redeemed himself the second year by becoming the top producer of draft mules.

Shortly thereafter, Washington similarly acquired two top-quality jennets and a smaller jack from Malta, which were sent to him by the Marquis de Lafayette. This jack, dubbed "The Knight of Malta," proved to be best suited for breeding with quality light horses to produce outstanding saddle mules.

October 26, 1785, marked the day that this future president's burning desire of a full-fledged breeding program for *an excellent race of mules* came to fruition. George Washington became *the* instrumental man in developing the mule into the best equine in the world, the American mule.

Man's Dependable Helping Hand

From that time on, these larger and stronger mules were right at home geeing and hawing on many farms in America. Vitally important jobs, such as working the soil, planting, harvesting, and pulling the crop-filled wagon to town for marketing, were the daily routine of many mules in service with man.

The extreme usefulness of these long-eared critters, with their developed skills and dependable nature, did not stop at the farm. These dedicated miracle workers dutifully helped in the building of roads, railroads, homes, and telephone and telegraph lines, to name just a few of their massive contributions. Mules also took part in creating some of the greatest engineering feats in America, including the building of the famous Los Angeles Aqueduct. Mules were the slaves' slaves as they pulled trolley cars in the cities and barges along the canals. Lumber camp and sawmill workers cherished the mules' endurance. Mules saw active duty in both world wars and the Civil War, where they carried food, supplies, and ammunition into battle zones and often carried the wounded out.

The mule could not be used for every conceivable purpose because of his natural reasoning ability (some call it "stubbornness"). History has it told that efforts were made to adapt mules to cavalry service on the front line of the war battlefield. The mule's tendency to dispute his handler's decision, to pause and make up his own mind in determining personal safety, sometimes conflicted with high-up orders given to the soldier in charge of the mule.

Photo courtesy of Katrina Walker, Wilson Creek Plowing Days, Wilson Creek, WA.

Mules were instrumental in the survival of mankind in the early years.
Mules also were an impeccable tool in America's development.

Just imagine, in the heat of intense fighting, where any movement could save or cost a soldier his life, the partner mule suddenly realizes that he might get hurt if he goes along with those silly orders, and quickly decides to bolt for the safety of his quarters! Ultimately this reasoning ability of the mule limited his military use on the front lines to hauling cannons in and transporting wounded or dead bodies out.

Some mining mules would rarely see the light of day, spending most of their short lives working in underground mines. All mules have an independent nature, think for themselves, and rarely will put themselves in a dangerous position. Normally these are great qualities; however, on occasion this would create some problems for man and his endeavors. The following is a recollection by Peter Nalle,[2] miner from 1949 to 1951, of the use of mining mules in Bonne Terre, Missouri.

We had mules working underground when I was there. People today don't believe it. These mules were big, strong and healthy. Most were good natured but one, Red, hated engineers. Probably an engineer treated him badly at one time. Mules have good memories. Red would go out of his way to kick a surveyor or kick over a transit.

I remember a long discussion in the manager's office with one of the battery locomotive salesmen. The salesman was trying to get the manager to junk the mules, go modern, and get battery-gathering locomotives. I was called in to help, and tabulated the discussion points below:

	MULES	LOCOS
Average Life in Years	20-25	20-25
Initial Cost	$25	$15,000
Operating Costs	$3/day Feed	$8/day for power and grease
Maintenance over 20 years	$25 Vet, $200 Blacksmith	$4,500 for 2 batteries, 1 rebuild
Ability to Detect Bad Ground	Good to very good	Nil
Ability to Operate Independently	With training - Good	Nil
Willingness to Work Overtime	Never	Excellent as long as battery lasts
Willingness to Take Overload	Never	Acceptable but possible damage

Mules did have an uncanny ability to detect bad ground. If they would not enter a slope or heading, one could be almost certain that it was not safe. We assumed that they had better hearing and could hear ground working that we could not. One could never make a mule do something he did not want to do. A double shift was impossible. Hauling more than a reasonable number of cars was always refused by the mule. The number depended on the grade and all the mules would be in agreement. They did have a strong union.

Since the mules were used in place of a gathering locomotive, the miner running the mucking machine at the face would load a car and send it off behind the unsupervised mule to the side track. At the side track, the mule would kick off the hook to the car, step aside and let the loaded car coast into the other loads. The mule would turn around, back up, and the man at the side track would hook up an empty, and the mule would take it back to the loader, kick off the hook, and the car would coast into where the men were working. The mule would stand by till the car was loaded and then take it back to the side track.

Unlike horses, if a long weekend came around, you could give them 3 days food and they would not eat themselves to death on the first day. In general, the miners treated their mules well because all jobs were on a bonus basis and an uncooperative mule could really spoil your bonus.

20-Mule Team—An Amazing Story

History's most dramatic recognized feat accomplished with the cooperative partnership between mules and man was the hauling of borax ore by twenty-mule teams in the 1880s. Below is an excerpt from an article published by the U.S. Borax Company, entitled "And the . . . TWENTY MULE TEAM ROLLED."

With a growing demand for borax, an economical method had to be devised for freighting borax ore from the mines in Death Valley's vast dry lake beds to the nearest railhead at Mojave. This consisted of 165 miles of raw, blistering temperatures—often running as hot as 130° in summer with desolate mountains and desert.

Photo by U.S. Borax Collection, Courtesy National Park Service, Death Valley National Park.

In the 1800s, the mule was the essential factor in transporting borax ore from mining camps to the railway depot. Twenty-mule teams are a rare sight today.

Experimenting, William T. Coleman found that twenty mules could move 36 tons with relative ease. The wagon beds were 16 feet long, four feet wide and six feet deep. Empty, each wagon weighed 7,800 pounds. The mule teams pulled two loaded wagons plus the iron water tanks that held 1,200 gallons [of water], making a total load of 73,200 pounds or over 36 tons.

Each twenty mule team crew consisted of only two men, a driver (called a muleskinner) and a swamper. They were usually silent, short-tempered men and the loneliness, monotony and hardships of their work made them no easier to get along with!

The muleskinner drove his team from the box of the first wagon or, in rough going, from the back of the nigh wheeler, the left-hand mule nearest the wheel. His only means of controlling the teams were his voice and the jerk line, a long rope that ran through the collar ring of each left-hand mule and attached to the leaders. A steady pull turned the team to the left, a series of jerks sent them to the right. Among many other tasks, the swamper helped apply the brakes on downgrades, cooked the meals, and unharnessed the mules each day.

From 1883 to 1889, the twenty mule teams hauled borax out of Death Valley to Mojave, traveling 15–18 miles a day, a 20 day round trip. During these years the twenty mule teams carried over 20 million pounds of borax out of the valley without a single breakdown—a considerable tribute to the ingenuity of the designers and builders and to the stamina of teamsters, swampers and mules.

John Spears, a *New York Sun* reporter in Death Valley in 1891, wrote about the life of a teamster driving the twenty-mule teams.

The life of a teamster on the desert is not only one of hardship, it is in places extremely dangerous. ...There are other grades, down the mountain, like the one, for instance, on the road from Granite Spring toward Mojave, where the plunge is not only steep, but the roadbed is as hard as a turnpike. The load must go down, and so when the brink is reached, the driver throws his weight on the brake of the front wagon. The swamper (assistant) handles the brake on the rear one, and away they go, creaking, and groaning, and sliding, til the bottom is reached. If the brake holds, all is well, but now and then a brake-block gives way, and such a race with death as then begins cannot be seen elsewhere. With yells and curses, the long team is started in a gallop, an effort is made to swing them around up the mountainside, a curve is reached, an animal falls, or a wheel strikes a rock or rut, and with a thunderous crash, over go the great wagon, and the teamster who has stuck with his post goes with them...[3]

J. C. Penney's Contribution

One other prominent person who needs to be mentioned regarding positive affiliations with the mule is J. C. Penney.

In 1938, Mr. Penney, founder of the J. C. Penney Company, bought a jack named Gold Dust because of his rare golden color. He was sold for $5,000 by Louis Monsees, a prominent jack and jennet breeder who owned Limestone Valley Farm near Smithton, Missouri. This was the highest price ever paid for a jack at that time. Mr. Penney, who at one time owned several thousand acres ...was considered one of the greatest livestock breeders of his generation and prominently identified with jack and jennet breeding.[4]

15

Photo courtesy of Marsha Arthur, Yerington, NV. Photo of Jim Porter, Spring Canyon Mule Makers, Onyx, CA.

Years ago, traveling was tremendously slower than today, but the quality of life was very rich.

The coming of the automobile and tractor directly affected the quantity of mules in America. This new invention, the gas engine, captivated Americans and turned their heads away from the mule. In 1960, the number of mules was extremely low, nearing the point of extinction. In recent years, intelligent man has again realized the immense value of the mule as a partner and has determinedly engineered the mule's comeback as a work and sport animal. The mule lives on!

CHAPTER 2:
TODAY'S MULE AS A SPORT ANIMAL

"YOU DO *WHAT* WITH YOUR MULE?"

It is amazing to learn of the vast applications mules are active in today. Whatever a horse can do, the mule has now been trained to do also. His versatility is an important factor for the increasing popularity of the American mule as a sport animal. I have asked people in authority how many mules there are in the United States today. Since there is no need to register a sterile animal, there is not an accurate count of the quantity. Mule enthusiasts know that mules are everywhere, performing competitively in all arenas and grazing inconspicuously on America's pastures. The non-mule person simply hasn't developed an eye for noticing those long ears and mealy noses in pastures yet!

Athletic Abilities Today

For many years, one has found mules in the mountains, where they are used as exceptional pack and riding animals for hunters and hikers. With their naturally calm nature, mules are also found hitched to parade wagons and farm equipment. Recently, the partnership of mule and man has taken a definite sporting direction. Mules are now found under saddle and harness, successfully performing any sporting event and competition imaginable. Let's take a look at some of these numerous activities in which mules participate and excel in the present day.

Endurance Riding—Mules naturally pace themselves appropriately to go the distance.

Pleasure Driving—From pulling single carts to multiple-hitch wagons, mules do it all.

Precision and Obstacle Driving—The independence of the mule, determinedly fearful of certain obstacles—yet only at certain times—makes for an interesting class to watch or participate in!

Chariot and Chuck Wagon Racing—These fast events generally consists of two or more mules pulling a lightweight chariot, or a small chuck wagon, manned by a fearless driver. The teams zip around a course in a timed race against other teams, watching closely to escape linking wheels with their competitors, or losing a wheel entirely.

Weight-Pulling Contests—Teams of draft mules compete to pull the maximum weight they can for their size.

Cow Cutting—The highly skilled cow ability of the mule is used on actual working ranches and also in arena competition.

Steer Stopping—Trained thoroughly, a mule may very well completely stop the steer, regardless of the rider's ability!

Cow Penning—This is a popular competitive sport of cutting a steer out of a group of three and herding it into a small fenced area within a time limit. The calm aura of the mule aids in keeping the steers in a relaxed frame of mind, so they are less apt to panic and scatter.

Calf Roping—Mules learn quickly to lay their ears flat out to the side when the roper swings the lariat in preparation to rope the running calf ahead. He certainly does not want that lariat to hit those sensitive ears!

Reining Competitions—The mule's natural limberness allows him to move quickly and turn tightly.

Photo courtesy of Nancy Hawthorn, Flying H Farm, Sims, AR. Nancy aboard Margo.

Mules excel in many horse activities. Mule, horse, dog, and riders tend to cattle on a real cattle drive.

Coon Hunting—Dismount and put your coat over the fence so the mule can see the wire height. Those trained coon-hunting mules will then jump willingly over the coat!

Packing Contests—Which team can pack the best and fastest? Packing contests also include the famous Bishop Mule Days Pack Scramble. This event is where several owners turn all their mules loose at once in a large arena. When a gun is sounded, owners scramble to catch their own mules (which can be the most interesting part of this event) and pack them with awkward, bulky items such as fifty-gallon empty barrels and large sheets of plywood. The first team of packed mules to shoot across the finish line with all items intact is dubbed the winner.

High-Country Travel—Hunters, hikers, outfitters, guides, and guests appreciate the stability in packing and riding the sure-footed mule in high, mountainous areas.

Jumping—Dual-faceted jumping includes cross-country jumping at a canter, as in horse competitions, and also bounding over jumps from a standing start, as in coon hunting.

Dressage—Mules are capable of learning even high-level dressage moves. Most mules seem to enjoy the mental challenge that dressage requires.

Combined Driving—This driving sport consists of a single mule or a team of mules pulling a cart and performing a three-fold event of dressage, marathon, and an obstacle course, all under harness.

English and Western Shows—Shows include conformation class, English- and Western-style riding, driving, and other basic classes, the same as you find at horse shows.

Pari-Mutual Racing—Mule racing is the same distance and style of racing as quarter horse racing, but with a greater risk of "spontaneous resistance" from the mule!

Speed Events—Barrel-racing, keyhole, and pole-bending competitions are a few of these speed events.

Gymkhanas—These include various games for fun and competition, such as goat tying, egg and spoon races, bed roll races, and musical tires.

Trail Riding—Pleasure and competitive riding in the hills, trees, mountains, and desert. ("There is nothing better than being on the back of my mule in the woods."—Author)

Plowing Contests—Mule teams compete with draft horses to see which team can plow the straightest, most consistent furrow.

Grand Canyon Trails—Mules have carried tourists and gear down the intimidating, cliff-edged trails of the Grand Canyon for an amazingly near-perfect 100 year safety record.

Photo courtesy of M. Allen Dawson, Midway, KY, www.pbase.com

One of the most noted jobs for mules in the southwest is packing dudes and their belongings down the wild Grand Canyon trails.

1976 Endurance Ride

The mule has great endurance and independence, and desires a working partnership with man. One of the most famous endurance rides, The Great American Horse Race, was held in 1976. The object was to take your favorite horse or mule, along with a backup mount, and the three of you trek clear across America, from the starting line in New York to the finish line in California. The first one to cross the finish line won the pot of money put up for this courageous event. Below is how Emerson Johnson recalls the race:

On Memorial Day 1976, 175 horses and 5 mules gathered for the start of the Great American Horse Race at the Herkimer County Fairgrounds in Frankfort, N.Y. The finish line was in Sacramento at the California Exposition Grounds 3,200 miles away. The 100 or so riders of both sexes and mixed ages, had all paid an entry fee of $500. The purse was $50,000 to be apportioned among the first 10 place winners. Each rider was permitted to lead a spare mount if he or she chose, and most of them did.

A 60 year old steeplejack and horse rancher from San Jose, California, named Virl Norton had posted his $500. He was as tough as the two mules he would be riding. His lead mule was Lord Fauntleroy, son of a thoroughbred mare and a mammoth jack. His spare mount, Lady Eloise, was of the same mixture. Both were dark brown and 16 hands high.

Ninety-eight days later, Norton pulled up before the battery of television cameras and reporters in Sacramento, winner by 9 hours and 17 minutes over the second place horse, an Arabian trotter! This was the equivalent of 75 miles by Norton's estimate. (Averaging 30 miles per day at a pace of 8.5 m.p.h.) A few of Norton's competitors complained about the way the race was run. Two maintained that if it had been a bit longer their horses would have won. Norton replied, 'Okay, give me 72 hours and we'll turn around and race back. We'll each put up $10,000, winner takes all'. No one stepped forward.

The mules each lost 150 pounds during the race. Norton lost 26. All arrived lean, hard, and well. Norton was richer by $25,000 and two western mules had made racing history. When those mules left New

21

Photo courtesy of Marsha Arthur, Yerington, NV. Marsha on partner, Annie Get Your Guns.

The sure footed mule is an excellent choice for safety, consistency, and reliability for trail and endurance competitions.

York, they were headed for their barn in San Jose. There are few places a mule would rather go than to the barn![5]

With imagination you can find endless activities in which your mule and you can partner to accomplish goals successfully. My imagination took me to a place I had never even previously considered. Sally (my molly mule) and I developed a comedy act, which we perform to show how wonderful mules are. Whatever you are able to do with a horse, you can do with your mule. It simply takes the proper training. The end result is that you may have an even better partner than the horse you were planning on training for this activity! Remember, a mule is capable of any activity you thought only a horse could do, except reproduce.

CHAPTER 3:
PROMINENT MULE LANDMARKS

"WHERE *IS* THE MULE CAPITAL OF THE WORLD?"

Man has valued the mule so much throughout the years that at one time there was fierce competition between several United States towns for the honored title "Mule Capital of the World." This competition for the title is still alive and well today. Who wouldn't want their town to be associated with the smartest equine worker, the most devoted sporting partner, and the best friend of the working man? Some of these geographic locales have special significance in the development of the mule. Below are a few of these locations so you may decide for yourself which place deserves this honored title. Let's first address Columbia, Tennessee, the ancestor of these competing towns.

Columbia, Tennessee

The durable mule was a dire necessity of daily life in the 1840s. Demand for quality work from mules was extremely high east of the Mississippi, stretching from the Canadian border all the way south to the Gulf of Mexico. Columbia, Tennessee, with its convenient central location, naturally became the crossroads of mule activity for both buyer and seller, in the form of street fairs.

Initially, these street fairs were called Breeder's Day. Folks traveled to Columbia from all directions to buy, trade, and sell the breeding service of their jack stock. The marketers soon developed a parade to visually display their jacks and to proudly show off the mules they had for sale. Viewing the animals' movements, temperament, and conformation aided the buyer in making an educated decision on his forthcoming purchase.

A similar festival has carried over in this Tennessee town. Today, this event is designated more appropriately as Mule Day. Rather than focusing on breeding stock and sales on this first Monday in April, the townsfolk arrange an annual celebration of the mule. Columbia's modern-day style of Mule Day began in 1932 and became an official event in 1934 until 1942. The event was then again recognized from 1947 to 1950, and has been a staple of Columbia each and every year since 1974.

Currently sponsored by the Maury County Bridle and Saddle Club, this mule event has shows, games, and pulling contests. The highlight of this event is a mile-long parade that honors the Queen Mule of the current year. The Queen (or King) Mule then has the honor of riding on the queen float with his or her human queen and attendants. In 1950, the Queen Mule float was pulled by a twenty-mule team. This parade does not allow any motorized vehicles except those pulling floats, and hosts over 200,000 wide-eyed observers at this annual event.

Today, Columbia is still noted for the largest mule sale in the world. The draft mules purchased mainly go to the Pennsylvania Amish for use on their farms. Some of the Columbia-sold mules go to Georgia and Florida for hauling bird hunters deep into the field by wagon. A small quantity of mules sold end up in Brazil, where these dependable workers earn their living by hauling coffee beans out of remote mountain areas. However, by far the largest quantity of riding mule stock sold is shipped to the West (plus all over the U.S.) for use in riding, competing, and recreation.

Other Tennessee Towns

The small community of Lynchburg, Tennessee, holds the honor of proclaiming October 26, 1985, as Mule Appreciation Day. On this day two hundred years ago, George Washington acquired jack stock and began a breeding program for the American mule (see Mules of the Past, Chapter 1). There was consideration throughout the country to proclaim each October 26 as Mule Appreciation Day, but the government of the United States

Photo courtesy of Reese Brothers Mule Company, Gallatin, TN.

Tennessee is famous for the largest mule auction in the world.

decided (and holds, to date) that it was not appropriate for the mule to have his own holiday.

Shelbyville, Tennessee, is traditionally the home of the five-gaited Tennessee Walking Horse. This town in central Tennessee hosts the hottest mule show east of the Mississippi, The Great Mule Celebration. Held in the summer, this three-day mule event is vast, versatile, and varied. The indoor show stems from mini to draft performances, from hunter-hack to dressage competitions, and all else in between. There are an estimated 500 skilled and beautiful mules attending the show, and over 10,000 mule enthusiasts. This event also has special classes specifically for the gaited mule. A gaited mule is any mule that has a smooth gait other than a walk, and not exactly a trot.

Missouri and Texas

Next on the list of landmarks for you to consider in your decision of the Mule Capital of the World are the states of Missouri and Texas—and here's why. Near the turn of the century, Missouri was tops in mule production. The first mules in Missouri came from Mexico in 1820. These were small mules that traveled via the Santa Fe Trail. The first European jacks in Missouri were brown Maltese jacks, brought up the Mississippi River to New Franklin, Missouri, in 1838.

In 1890 the Missouri mule population reached 245,273, the highest ranked of all states according to U.S. Census figures. Texas took the lead in 1900 with 474,737 and reached a high in 1930 of 1,040,106. In 1922 there were 440,000 mules in Missouri, however the number dropped to an all time low of 75,000.[6]

Texans hoarded their mules for themselves, realizing how beneficial they were. Missouri breeders sold and shipped their stock throughout the world in response to others in need of a great beast of burden. The British army used Missouri mules exclusively in World War I. Missouri obtained most of their jack stock from Kentucky and gained fame for mule breeding.

Bishop, California

The most mentionable mule town in the West is Bishop, California. This town of approximately 3,500 folks is a quaint resort community in the high Sierras, approximately 300 miles northeast of Los Angeles. This lush Owens Valley town is surrounded by dry, mountainous hills. Each year on Memorial Day weekend in May, the town lights up and the population grows to approximately 30,000 people and over 700 mules. This five-day mule extravaganza features Bishop Mule Days and has just about every type of mule competition the mind can imagine.

Bishop Mule Days originated in 1970 to honor the mule and acknowledge his prowess in pleasure, sport, and competition. Today a full slate of competitive events is featured, including events such as barrel racing, calf roping, steer stopping, cow penning, flat racing, and carriage driving. Activities also range from packing to dressage, and from team chariot racing to mule-shoeing contests. Of course there is a show division with western and English pleasure classes and donkey and mule halter classes. But the show doesn't stop there, as there are social events to carry you through five days of unique entertainment, including concerts with known musicians, a wild and crazy dance, the well-known and well-attended barbecue, a mule auction to die for, and simply shootin' the breeze with the friendliest equine folks you will find anywhere!

Photo courtesy of Bill Vassar, www.vassarphotography.com.

Pari-mutual racing is a popular event around the country;
and a fan favorite at Bishop Mule Days.

Mules in the United Kingdom

Word about the mule as a superior sport animal has reached other nations as well. With the wonders of the Internet, I learned that the British have a mule organization, too! The British Mule Society was founded in 1978 by Lorraine Travis. The purpose of this group is to preserve, improve, and promote the mule, along with an emphasis on the prevention of cruelty. Each summer these folks host a British Mule Days, featuring mules from all over the country that compete in riding, driving, and in-hand classes.

Mule-Named Places

The versatility of the mule, along with his independent nature, has prompted many places to carry the mule name. Some of them are below.

The mule is the army's mascot at the United States Academy at West Point because of his "strength, heartiness and perseverance," which is symbolic of the cadets.

Jackassville is in Siskiyou County, California.

Mad Mule Gulch can be found in Shasta County, California.

Crazy Mule Gulch is in Yosemite National Park, California.

Deadhorse is a town at Prudhoe Bay in Alaska. Prospectors in the gold rush days came to this area using horses as their beasts of burden. They managed just fine during the summer, but the rugged north Alaska winters depleted the horse stock and the prospectors came to realize that the hardier mules served them better on a year-round basis because of their natural ability to handle extreme temperatures.

Gray Mule is a ghost town located in Floyd County up in the Texas panhandle. Gray Mule was a thriving community in the 1920s that included a cotton gin, schoolhouse, blacksmith shop, and even a baseball diamond.

There it is folks, pertinent information for *you* to decide on the Mule Capital of the World.

CHAPTER 4:
MULE AND DONKEY TERMS AND VARIATIONS

"MY MULE MARE HAD A MARE MULE YESTERDAY!"

Folks introduced to the mule and donkey world quickly become overwhelmed at the entourage of terms available for their beloved long-eared friends. In talking to mule owners I have heard many of the following terms applied at one time or another for the same animal. Seems the old timers have their personal mule and donkey vocabulary, as do the folks in the east, south, and west portions of the nation. Let's try to make some sense out of these terms in our efforts to produce a consistent longears language for clearer communication and better understanding.

Common Mule Terms

Below are some of the numerous terms for the mule. The underlined terms are the most common and appropriate, and are used throughout this book.

MULE: The offspring of a donkey jack and a horse mare. Some say this cross is the most successful hybrid ever developed.

JOHN MULE: The male mule that has been gelded. Although sterile, male mules can have obnoxious stallion tendencies and therefore are always gelded when young.

JACK MULE: The male mule that has not been gelded. Basically, the term "jack mule" is used to distinguish between a gelded mule and an intact mule. Rarely does one find intact (or jack) mules.

HORSE MULE: A term used for a male mule.

HORSE COLT: Old timers' term for a male mule foal.

<u>**MOLLY MULE**</u>: A female mule. She comes in heat as a horse mare does but rarely conceives, as she is usually sterile (for exceptions, see Sexuality and Fertility of the Mule, Chapter 5).

MARE MULE: A female mule (see Molly Mule).

MULE MARE: A horse broodmare who mates with a donkey jack to produce mules.

MULE SKINNER: Driver of a multiple hitch of mules. In the 1850s to 1870s, millions of tons of freight were pulled by mules or oxen. Rumor has it that the drivers of these lengthy teams used a long leather whip which could take the skin off a mule.

Mules of Size

In days past, where mules were primarily used as man's beast of burden, the mule was named for his size and for the work that he was most capable of doing. Below are terms currently used for the mule, ranging from small to large. Again, the most appropriate terms used today are underlined. Note that a hand is 4 inches.

<u>**MINIATURE MULE:**</u> Height ranging up to 36 inches at the withers. These mules are bred from miniature mares or pony mares and are usually crossed with miniature Mediterranean jacks.

PONY MULE: Another name for a miniature mule.

MINE MULE: Small mule used to work in the mine shafts in the mid-1900s (see Mules of the Past, Chapter 1). Today, this term signifies a miniature size of mule.

Photo courtesy of Luanne Hott, Oakbrooke Farm, Wartrace, TN.

Miniature mules are great for pulling lightweight wagons and for showing. Luanne Hott proudly parades Miniscule's Lil Jack Squat around the show ring.

COTTON MULE: Any type of mule that is 14 to 15 hands, and that weighs from 750 to 1,100 pounds. This mule was used extensively in the cotton and tobacco fields of yesteryear.

LIGHT MULE or <u>SADDLE MULE</u>: The saddle mule is the most common term for a mule bred out of a mare of any of the light horse breeds and crossed with a mammoth or standard jack.

SUGAR MULE: A sugar mule is the old timers' term for a mule formerly used in the sugar farming industry. Sugar mules are larger than cotton mules, but smaller than draft mules. They generally run 1,100 to 1,200 pounds and are 14.2 to 15.2 hands tall.

<u>DRAFT MULE</u>: A draft mule that is bred out of a mare of the draft horse breeds. Draft mule size usually runs 15 to 17 hands or better, weighing in at 1,200 to 1,600 pounds.

Common Donkey Terms

To better understand the mule, we first must identify his father, the donkey. The following terms are applied to donkeys, with the proper terms underlined and used throughout this book.

EQUUS ASINUS: This is the scientific name for the complete breed of donkey. This is how the term "ass" was derived, and many jokes have blossomed.

ASS: Slang term for donkey that was used in biblical times and is still used in regard to the current wild asses of Asia and Africa.

JACK or **JACKASS:** A jack is a stallion (intact) donkey. This is the current-day term for all breeding male donkeys.

GELDING: As in the horse and mule world, gelding is the proper term to designate a gelded male donkey.

HE-ASS or SHE-ASS: Male or female donkey, respectively.

BURRO: Spanish word for donkey. This term is usually intended for the smaller-sized donkey (9 to 12 hands), but is also used interchangeably with the term "donkey."

DONKEY: This is the current-day term for the ass. This term has been adopted from breeders to designate a gelded male. However, all asses can be considered donkeys. In this book, "donkey" is used as a generic term for both the male and female ass.

JACK STOCK: Plural term for stallion (intact) donkeys that are used for breeding.

JENNY or **JENNET** (jen' it): A female donkey.

Donkeys of Size

Donkeys are primarily distinguished by their height. With the aid of *The Modern Mule*[7] by Paul and Betsy Hutchins, below are the standards for the American Donkey and Mule Society (ADMS). All height measurement is from the ground to the top of the withers, sometimes noted in inches, sometimes noted in hands (1 hand equals 4 inches).

MINIATURE DONKEY: A donkey that is less than 36 inches tall.

SMALL STANDARD DONKEY: Between 36 and 48 inches, measured at the withers.

LARGE STANDARD DONKEY: 48 inches up to mammoth size.

MAMMOTH DONKEY: 54 inches or 13.2 hands minimum for the jennet, and 56 inches or 14 hands-plus for the jack in height; at least 7 inches around the smallest part of the cannon bone, between the donkey's front ankle and the knee.

Donkey Breeds

As with most any animal, there are specific breeds of the donkey. The jacks used for breeding in the United States quite commonly are not one specific breed, but a combination of the breeds listed below. Here are a few of the recognized donkey breeds, taken from an article by the late, Dick Spencer, "Probably More Than You Ever Wanted to Know About Mules,"[8]

Spanish Donkey: A universal term applied to designate the burro, which originates from Spain. The Spanish jack (as you will hear the breeding males referred to) is often a cross between a burro and the mammoth stock. This cross gives the donkey ample bone, size, and agility, as well as refinement. Some types below are specific breeds of the Spanish donkey.

Catalonian: Considered by some to be the finest of jack stock. The most horse-like of all the donkey breeds, the Catalonian donkey originated in the Catalonia province of the Pyrenees of Spain. They are usually 14 to 16 hands high, very leggy, and light-bodied, with flat, clean bone, style, and action. The predominant color is black with white points; however, they are occasionally gray or brown.

Andalucian: Found in southern Spain, these donkeys are large in size, reaching 15 hands, with well-shaped legs and large, firm bone. They have good dispositions and are usually gray or roan. This is the donkey breed

Photo courtesy of Rory Wallis, Nerja Donkey Sanctuary, Province of Malaga, Spain.

The striking Andalucian donkey was the chosen breed brought over to America, courtesy of George Washington.

that George Washington used for his initial breeding for draft mules (see Mules of the Past, Chapter 1).

Majorcan: Originating from the resort island of Majorca of the Balearic Islands in the Mediterranean, these donkeys are rangier and a bit taller than the Catalonian donkeys. The Majorcan donkeys carry large bone and body and are black in color.

Maltese: These donkeys are a bit smaller, averaging 14 hands, and are very active breeders. They have well-shaped ears, heads, and bodies. Coat colors are mainly brown, but red, black, and grulla are also permissible. Used for the breeding of saddle mules, the Maltese donkey is the jack stock brought to America by the Spaniards (see Mules of the Past, Chapter 1).

Poitou: Originating in France, these donkeys are somewhat a rarity in the United States. Once you have seen one you won't forget it, as they have very long hair on the neck, ears, and legs. The head and body are also very shaggy. They average around 15 hands and are the biggest, coarsest donkeys to be found in terms of their bone and body. They have good feet, a large head, and large eyes.

Sicilian: Originating from Sicily, these are the smaller donkeys that are used for the breeding of miniature donkeys and mules intended for the use of cart driving, or simply for pets. They are generally under 9 hands, with coloring of gray or brown.

Italian: These donkeys from Italy are 12.2 to 14 hands, with good bone and feet.

Registries and Acronyms

There are several registries of the mule and donkey. Among them are the following:

ADMS: American Donkey and Mule Society (www.lovelongears.com)— established 1967. This is the umbrella organization which houses the following six registries:

- **ADR:** American Donkey Registry—established 1967, for donkeys of all sizes.

- **MDR:** Miniature Donkey Registry—established 1958.

- **AMR:** American Mule Registry—established 1967.

- **AMRR:** American Mule Racing Registry.

- **Zebra Hybrid/Bloodstock Registry**—established 1997, for zebra hybrids and their purebred breeding stock parents.

- **The North American Baudet du Poitou Society**—established 1995, for pure and part-bred Poitou donkeys.

ACOSA: American Council of Spotted Asses, Inc. (http://spottedass.com) —a color registry only. Donkeys must be visibly spotted to qualify for this registry.

AMA: American Mule Association (www.americanmuleassociation.com)— registers mules and some jackstock of these mules.

AMJR: American Mammoth Jackstock Registry, formerly the Standard Jack and Jennet Registry (www.amjr.us)—they register jackstock only, no mules.

AMRA: American Mule Racing Association (www.muleracing.org).

CDMA: Canadian Donkey and Mule Assoc. (www.donkeyandmule.com) —the only national registry and association for donkeys and mules in Canada.

IMDR: International Miniature Donkey Registry—established 1992 (www.qis.net/~minidonk/imdr.htm).

NASMA: North America Saddle Mule Association (www.nasma.us)—this family association houses mule and donkey registrations, records points for showing, and gives out cool prizes for high-point winners and placers!

NMDA: National Miniature Donkey Association (www.nmdaasset.com)— not a registry, but a prominent showing association for miniature donkeys.

Hinny

As you know, a mule is a cross between a mare (female horse) and a jack (intact male donkey). Now, when you reverse that combination and breed a stallion (intact male horse) to a jenny (female breeding donkey), what you get, if you are lucky, is an animal called a hinny. Hinnies are also sterile, as are mules. Both mules and hinnies have an inappropriate number of chromosomes to successfully reproduce. Those bodies within the sex cells must pair up evenly to produce offspring. A donkey has sixty-two chromosomes and a horse has sixty-four. Combining these two species, both the mule and the hinny chime in with sixty-three chromosomes. In layman's language, an odd number of chromosomes is the technical reason for sterility in both hybrids.

If you find an animal that looks very similar to a mule, but something isn't exactly right, and you know he is *not* a donkey and definitely not a pony, either—consider the possibility that this equine could be a hinny.

Quite often hinnies are white in color and smaller in size than a mule, due to their mother being the smaller parent. However, hinnies *can* come in any

Photo by Cynthia Attar, author.

The hinny looks very much like a mule, but with a few additional horse-like characteristics. Harmony Farm's Ivan helps to educate people on the differences between a hinny and a mule.

size and color. Some hinnies look so surprisingly similar to a mule that they are mistaken for one. Even judges of mule events and longtime mule enthusiasts—including me—are hard pressed to distinguish hinnies from mules.

Recently I went to look at a hinny to bring onto Harmony Farm to use as an equine education tool. When I arrived to view Ivan, I wasn't convinced he actually was a hinny. Since he was a rescue guy, his parentage was unknown. I initially concluded that he was a white mule. When I got home and researched hinnies on the Internet, I could detect that Ivan possessed slight differences that convinced me he was a hinny and not a mule—most notably, his unusual bray! I eventually brought Ivan home, and he now graces Harmony Farm in hinny style. He, Sally the WonderMule, and Satchmo the jazzy donk, now teach people and kids about equines and equine hybrids.

Upon closer evaluation in comparison to a mule, the hinny reveals a slightly rounder barrel and shapelier round rear end, like his father the horse. The hinny ear is usually not quite as long as the mule ear, and it possesses a wider chest and straighter legs. In short, a hinny looks just a bit more like a horse than does his brother the mule.

"Mare hinny" is the proper term for a female, and "horse hinny" is the proper term for a gelded male. Again, since hinnies are sterile, there is no sense in keeping an intact male hinny and all the challenges that brings with it.

Natural breeding for hinnies is difficult for both the stallion horse and the jenny, and therefore hinnies are a bit harder to come by. The stallion quite often simply refuses to breed to a donkey, and if you find one who will accept a jenny, the jenny may have a tendency to abort the foal. When breeding for a hinny, one needs to be aware of the possibility of disfiguring a jenny to be swaybacked for life when a much larger and heavier stallion mounts for breeding and the bigger foal is carried to term. The following article regards an official study at Cambridge and Cornell University on breeding for hinnies:

> During a seven year period in two laboratories (Cambridge and Cornell University) a total of 159 attempts were made in successive breeding seasons to establish hinny pregnancies in 51 jenny donkeys. These jennies appeared to be of normal fertility and were cycling normally and ovulating regularly. A total of 6 pony and horse stallions, all of proven high fertility, were used with a mixture of natural mating and artificial insemination on alternate days during estrous.
>
> In 25 instances, the mated/inseminated jenny donkey was left untouched in the hope of establishing a normal ongoing hinny pregnancy; this occurred in 18 cases to give a conception rate of only 14.4%.[9]

Today the hinny seems to be as smart as the mule, and some say they are faster and friendlier than a horse. However, others say that their intelligence is not worth much and they have no useful purpose. Even at only 14.4 percent success rate in breeding for hinnies, the near future should provide us more information about them. You know people; whatever is unusual and hard to come by, they want!

Onager

With the help of *Wild Horses: A Spirit Unbroken*, by Elwyn Hartley Edwards,[10] and the Internet, I will help to clarify the other living wild species of the horse, commonly called the onager—or specifically, the *Equus hemionus*. Hemionid means half-ass, and is used to describe an animal having the nature and characteristics of both the horse and the ass, but that is not a cross between the two (as is a mule).

The kulan (*Equus hemionus*), a nearly extinct wild ass, can still be found today traveling the Gobi Desert in Mongolia in Western Asia. A subspecies called the kiang (*Equus hemionus kiang*) climb the rocky Tibetan plateaus and are sacred to the Tibetans, so they are not hunted.

In India, the Indian onager (*Equus hemionus khur*) still exists in Rann of Kutch, near Pakistan. The kuhr was nearly extinct in the 60s, but it has made a slight comeback today.

The Persian onager (*Equus hemionus onager*), which is the ass spoken of in the Bible, is extinct in the wild today, as is the Syrian wild ass (*Equus hemionus hemippus*).

Przewalski's horse (*Equus przewalski*) is also known as the Mongolian wild horse. These descendents of horses were extinct in the wild for thirty years; however, with the help of zoos and hand breeding, they now have been reintroduced at Khustain Nuruu National Park in Mongolia.

Zebra

The next species is known as *Equus zebrus*. Of course we all know the zebra as the boldly black-and-white-striped, horse-like animal that we in America usually see only in a zoo or on a wildlife safari. There are three wild varieties of the zebra: the Grevy's, found in Ethiopia, Kenya, and Somali; the Burchell's (or Plains) zebra in east and southeast Africa; and the Hartmann's Mountain Zebra, originating from South Africa. These three varieties can be identified by the arrangement of their stripes. For an in-depth study on zebras, wild asses, and wild horses, check the Suggested Readings at the end of this book.

Photos courtesy of Spectrum Ranch, Neshkoro, WI.

Zebra hybrids (or zebroids) are fascinating. On the left is a Zedonk foal, on the right is a zorse.

Zebroid

The generic name for any offshoot of the zebra/equine cross is "zebroid." In most cases, the stallion is any of the zebra species, mated with a horse mare. "Zorse," "zebra mule," and "zebrule" are terms applied for this cross.

When a stallion zebra is mated with a jenny donkey, the resulting cross is termed "zedonk," "zebronkey," "zebradonk," and "zonkey." Now, there is such a thing as the stallion/jack donkey mating with the zebra mare. This cross is considered a "zebrinny."

Zebroids will generally resemble their non-zebra parent, yet have only specific areas on their body (legs and/or head and neck) that are zebra-striped. The offspring in all of these cases are also sterile.

There are more and more of these colorful creatures in the U.S. Some are successfully trained; some will never be domesticated. I observed a zonkey at a horse demonstration. The handler had a tough time keeping him under control. This could have been a training problem, or it could be that this particular animal, like the zebra, is determinedly wild. Again, when more zebroids are produced, more information will be available.

INTERMEDIATE SECTION

IMPORTANT MULE FACTS

CHAPTER 5:
SEXUALITY AND FERTILITY
OF THE MULE

"WHICH IS BETTER, A JOHN MULE OR A MOLLY MULE?"

When it comes to mules, the lay person generally has many initial questions regarding these unusual four-legged equines before he can hold a greater appreciation of them. Here are a few of the most asked—and answered—questions from non-mule people.

- "Now, what is a mule, anyway?"— It's half-donkey, half-horse.

- "What's the difference between a donkey and a mule?"—A donkey is smaller, with longer ears.

- "Do they have male and female mules?"—Absolutely.

- "Can a mule reproduce?"—No, but she thinks she can.

- "What do you do with a mule?"—Anything you want and he agrees to!

It is amazing how nature accepts inter-species mating of the horse and donkey, but draws a line when it comes to allowing the offspring, the mule, to be fertile and to reproduce. At least you will never find an inbred mule! For your information, the gestation of a horse foal is eleven months, the gestation of a donkey foal is twelve to thirteen months, and the gestation of a mule foal is eleven to twelve months.

Sexual Preference

As far as the purchase of a mule, one question invariably arises. "Which is the better mule to own—the john mule or the molly mule?" This question nearly always creates a lively discussion between mule enthusiasts. In truth, there is no single answer to this question. As with horse owners, this answer is definitely a personal preference of the mule owner. Just remember, the individual mule you choose should first and foremost have the right attitude, long before the consideration of gender.

In the selling market, it seems that the mule's attitude and training, more than its gender, is what brings in the higher dollar. In Buying the Ideal Mule, Chapter 8, we look further into this subject.

Molly mules seem to be found in many of the mule hitches. Some owners attest the molly to be safer and more trustworthy, with a lower likelihood of getting headstrong. Some folks say that the molly seems to have just a bit more personality in her style. If that is true, it could possibly be explained because she possesses all her natural faculties.

Some folks thoroughly believe in the john mule, as they say he is more

Photo courtesy of Bob Bellinger, Pendleton, SC.

This john mule pulls a carriage for hire around the city with ease.

predictable and even-tempered. These people may not own a molly because of her moodiness, created by the female cycle. Then on the other hand, some say the john mule may lose more pizzazz or life in his step than a horse gelding. (I have not found this to be true.) Both have the potential to be a great partner and worker for their handler. Again, the sex of your mule is a personal preference, and the mule's great attitude should be your ultimate prime concern.

Mollys in Season and Jack Mules

Both the molly mule and the jack mule (intact male) have the same sexual desires as the horse or donkey. Yes, mollys do come in and out of season, just the same as their half-sister, the horse mare. Some molly seasons are obvious and regular, and some are barely noticeable.

A molly in season reacts in a similar manner as a mare, namely with the action that breeders term "squat and pee." This is where they somewhat squat with their hind legs and look as though they are going to urinate, but very little is discharged, and what does trickle out usually is a small amount of creamy fluid. This is a natural action of the horse mare, telling the stallion she is ready for breeding.

From the donkey side, the molly may also have another behavior when in season, a sort of chewing motion with her mouth, similar to a foal trying to make friends with an older horse. With head stretched out and the lips pulled back, the foal tells others in the herd that he is submissive to them and below them on the pecking order. With jennies (donkeys), this mouthing action is coupled with a humping of the back, and is another way to tell the jack she is ready for breeding.

If you are as unlucky as I am, you will have a mule that reacts in both ways. One winter when my molly mule, Sally, was housed near a horse colt, she decided she would come into season every third Saturday—my main riding day. On these days, Sally would just stand there solid when I mounted and then gave that squat and pee stance. When I worked her out of that reflex, she would then hump her back and chew with her mouth, I was able to work her out of this instinct as well; however, I knew not to schedule classes at that time or expect an abundance of willingness from her! Sally was excessive in this instinct, as most mollies won't react quite this

Photo courtesy of SAU Communications, Magnolia, AR.

Both john and molly mules are highly capable animals. Molly B displays her expertise on jumping from a standing start.

determinedly. Her strong drive was mainly due to the influence of a stallion colt nearby. When not housed near a stallion or jack, Sally rarely comes into season.

Just keep in mind that mollies will show their heat cycles more frequently and strongly if housed near a stallion horse or a jack donkey. Horse mares do not come into season in the cold, frigid winter months. Since the gestation of a horse foal is eleven months, this is nature's way of preventing the young from being born when there is little feed (grass) available. Horse mares will come into season monthly beginning in the springtime and up until the early winter. My experience is that that is not necessarily the case with molly mules. The most frequent time that I have found Sally in season is in the dead of winter—another one of those mule mysteries!

Adult jack mules have a tendency to be rank and aggressive, obviously ignoring the fact that they cannot reproduce. The mule, with his natural headstrong nature, can be a menace when kept as an intact jack mule. He is dangerous to have amongst horses because he may charge a male horse, and if he feels threatened, he can bite, tear, and kick a horse to pieces. The jack mule may force his way through or over anything and everyone to get at a mare in season. Since reproduction is out of the question with a mule anyway, the logical solution to these problems is to geld the male when he is very young. This allows for a very manageable and desirable working partner—the john mule.

Fertility

Is the mule a man-made animal? That is, do donkeys and horses naturally mate in the wild, or has their existence been solely dependent upon man's intervention? Well, I had always believed that this hybrid was strictly a product of man assisting the mating until I chatted with Kelly Grissom, a woman from the Bureau of Land Management (BLM). Apparently, there are a few naturally bred wild mules roaming around on BLM lands in the West. I saw two of these wild mules that had been captured. They stood about 13 hands tall and were quite attractive.

The fertility status of a mule, as mentioned, is that all mules are sterile. In the past, there have been reports of mules giving birth. Mostly the reports quoted are believed to be cases where the mule adopted an orphan colt of a mare in the same field, or just plain stole the foal from his mother. Another possibility is that the foaling mare was actually a horse that had some physical mule characteristics, and therefore was mistaken as a mule.

But whatever ironclad rule we all decide to agree upon, there are exceptions to prove us humans wrong! There had been no recorded proof of a mule giving birth until a few years back. In July of 1984, a foal was born to a molly mule named Krause, owned by Bill and Oneta Silvester in Champion, Ohio. This mule foal was dubbed "Blue Moon" for its rarity. In 1986, Krause proudly showed off her second offspring, "White Lightning," of the same type. Both of these foals were born with 63 chromosomes (making them mules and also sterile), and are the first scientifically documented mule foals born out of a molly mule. A jack named Chester proudly serves as the sire of both Blue Moon and White Lightning.

In 1990, Jim and Dinah Anderson of Mendenhall, California, noted that their fat molly mule gave birth to a male colt out of a quarter horse stallion. They named him Agiba, "miracle" in Egyptian.

Photo courtesy of Laura Amos, Winterhawk Outfitters, Collbran, CO.

In 2007, outfitters Larry and Laura Amos were surprised to discover their molly mule, Kate, had apparently given birth to a mule colt.

Another miracle mule foaling came from a molly mule named Kate, owned by Larry and Laura Amos of Collbran, Colorado. This mule was pastured in a herd of equines that included a jack donkey. Kate was sold to the Amos's to be used as a pack mule. Little did they know that the new mule in the pack string was miraculously pregnant—until she foaled a colt mule in the fall of 2007. With a jack as his father, Winterhawk Kule Mule Amos has the coloring of his sire. The list will probably go on with these exceptions to the rule.

Twins

Rarely, but more often than one would expect, horse mares deliver twin mule foals. It is time for a celebration if both twins are alive and healthy. On the other hand, this birth poses a life-threatening situation for the mare, as she generally has a lack of nutrients to sustain two fetuses. The stronger twin, usually the female, may consume most of the mare's nutrients, causing the second to be stunted. Quite often both twins are female because they are the stronger sex. Because the twins are mules, they are naturally stronger

and better able to grow on less nourishment than horse twins. Mule trainer
Meredith Hodges gives us insight to twin birth difficulties:

> *In a dog, cat, or animal given to litters, the uterus contracts in*
> *segments at birth to allow each baby an opportunity to line up for birth.*
> *In equines, the uterus contracts as a whole, often creating both foals to*
> *be pushed into the birth canal together. This usually ends in disaster.*[11]

CHAPTER 6:
MULE COLORS EXPLAINED

KEEPING COLORS SIMPLE

Question: How do you tell which one is the mule in a field of distant horses? **Answer:** Look for the white or mealy nose which stands out in a herd of solid horse noses!

With the help of Ben Green's *The Color of Horses*[12] and veterinarian Phillip Sponenberg's *Horse Color*,[13] I will attempt to integrate the information in these two fine books to explain the three basic categories of color found on the mule: intense colors, self colors, and other colors. One can get easily confused when studying the multitude of horse colors. Mules don't seem to come in nearly as many color variations, thank heavens! The purpose of this chapter is to clarify, not confuse, so we can readily identify a mule color upon sight. My goal is to be able to pay a compliment, such as "That's a nice-looking chestnut mule," without getting into an argument over whether it's a chestnut or a sorrel mule.

The first category of mule colors we will discuss is intense colors—brown/black, bay, dun, grulla, and grey. The second category is self colors—chestnut and sorrel. And lastly, the remainder of mule colors and other valuable information is collected under the heading "Other Colors." Color points on the mule mean the coloring in the mane, tail, ears, and lower legs.

Intense Colors

Brown/black, bay, dun, grey, and grulla are considered intense colors for the mule. These colors have a dark-colored hide under the hairs. Intense colors are generally more durable than the lighter-colored hides found in self colors. These colors have a history of withstanding more abuse from saddles, weather, and disease. The hairs of the intense colors do have a tendency to fade in climates with intense sun, however.

Some mules inherit a dorsal stripe (a horizontal stripe down the backbone) from their father, the jack. Some mules inherit both a dorsal stripe and a shoulder stripe (a vertical stripe down the shoulder on both sides of the body). This double-stripe combination is called by many names, such as Christ's cross, Maltese cross, or shoulder cross.

BROWN/BLACK: A black mule is coal black with no white anywhere. Not a lot of mules fall into this category, so brown/black is the accepted color for the dark mule which has consistent black or dark brown hairs throughout most of his features.

Photo courtesy of Shannon Garnaat, Liberty Hill Farm, Natural Dam, AR.

Elvira from Liberty Hill Farm is a good representation of the brown/black mule—very dark in nearly all parts of the body.

Body: The body of the brown/black mule is dark brown to coal black.

Mane and Tail: Mane and tail are the same dark color as the body.

Ears: Ear color is the same as body color.

Eye Area: The eye area usually is the same color as the body color. However, a brown/black can have a lighter shade circling the eye.

Lower Nose: The nose can be anywhere from the mule's body color to a lighter shade of the same color (also known as a "mealy nose"). Only occasionally will you find a true white coloring on the nose of the brown/black.

Inner Legs and Underbelly: The true black mule will have the same color underbelly and inner legs as body color. A brown/black will likely have white or lighter coloring in these areas.

Lower Legs: The lower legs will be the same as the body color.

Hooves: Black hooves in all cases.

BAY: The bay is the most durable of the mule colors. A bay mule is basically the same coloring as a bay horse—with the points of the lower legs, ear rims, mane, and tail being black. Some bays proudly carry the desirable shoulder cross.

Body: A bay's body color is from light brown to dark brown, from red to a reddish tint.

Mane and Tail: The mane and tail are black in all cases.

Ears: Black points are generally seen on the tips and edges of the ears.

Eye Area: The bay mule usually hosts light brown circles around the eyes, a bit lighter than the body color.

Lower Nose: A white or mealy nose is a typical bay feature.

Photo courtesy of Shannon Garnaat, Liberty Hill Farm, Natural Dam, AR.

Roberta from Liberty Hill Farm parades her bay coloring exquisitely. Note the black on the legs, mane, and tail; and the typical bay white points on the nose and inner legs.

Inner Legs and Underbelly: Usually the same or lighter coloring than the body; the inner legs and underbelly occasionally are white.

Lower Legs: Black lower legs in all cases—a traditional bay feature.

Hooves: Black hooves in all cases.

DUN or BUCKSKIN: The terms "dun" and "buckskin" are used interchangeably. This mule has light brown or cream-colored hair combined with a black dorsal stripe (required if the mule is to be considered a dun or buckskin), and quite frequently with a shoulder cross. Black, horizontal, zebra-like stripes can be visible on the ears and the legs. Typical black points found in the bay also apply to the dun.

Body: Cream to blond body hair color.

Mane and Tail: Black mane and tail in all cases.

Ears: Black on the tips of the ears, sometimes combined with black horizontal zebra stripes.

Photo courtesy of Donnie Oldham, Rockin O Mules, Shawnee, OK.

Cool Hand Luke from Rockin "O" Mules proudly shows off his zebra stripes on his legs. Many duns carry stripes on the ears, always a dorsal stripe, and they generally host a complete shoulder cross.

Eye Area: Same as the body color.

Nose: From mealy to white is acceptable on the lower nose.

Inner Legs and Underbelly: The darker the body color, the more likely the dun will have the same dark color on the inner legs and underbelly. If the dun mule is very light in color, he may have white on these areas.

Lower Legs: Black lower legs. Some mules have horizontal black zebra stripes on all or some lower legs.

Hooves: Black hooves in all cases.

GREY: As with horses, the grey mule carries a black hide with a mixture of black and white hairs, making the overall body color look as though it is grey. As a foal, the black hairs are dominant, and the grey mule is quite striking with his salt-and-pepper coloring. As the mule ages, the white hairs will reach a higher percentage than the black hairs, and the mule's color gradually becomes lighter and whiter throughout his years.

Photo courtesy of Melanie Wilson, Sagebrush Mules, Iberia, MO.

Colonel's Jack Frost from Sagebrush Mules is a good representation of the grey mule. Note his vast dappling. Greys lighten in color as they age, eventually turning completely white.

Body: Most shades of grey—from dark grey to white—possibly with dapples.

Mane and Tail: The grey carries a black mane and tail. This also can be a mixture of white and black hairs in a salt-and-pepper coloring.

Ears: Black hairs on the tips and edges of the ears.

Eye Area: If the mule's head is grey, circles around the eyes are usually lighter to white. If the head is white, the eye area will be white also.

Lower Nose: White or a light nose is typical for the grey.

Inner Legs and Underbelly: Usually the same color as the body is found in the inner legs and underbelly, occasionally with some white areas in these parts.

Lower Legs: The lower legs are black in most cases. Older grey mules may have a higher percentage of white on the body, including the legs.

Hooves: Black hooves in all cases.

GRULLA: A slate-blue or gray-mouse color with black points, as in the dun. Both the grulla and the dun may have white on the belly, inner hind legs, and flanks. The grulla usually has both a shoulder stripe and a dorsal stripe and may also have black zebra stripes over the knees and hocks.

Self Colors

Self colors encompass the many shades of red found in the sorrel and chestnut mules. All of the self colors are recessive to the above intense colors. This means that if one parent of breeding stock is an intense color and one parent is a self color, the offspring will usually follow the intense parent and result in an intense-colored offspring. Self colors bred to each other will usually produce self colors rather than intense colors.

Self colors seem to not have quite the durability and resistance in the hair and hide that you find in the intense colors. Self colors tend to be more affected by heat, sweat, and pressure; therefore, saddles and harnesses may

Photo courtesy of Heather Wells, 7 Lazy K Quarter Horses, Boulder, WY.

Eddie from 7 Lazy K Quarter Horses displays typical chestnut markings. The body, mane, and tail color is the same throughout the body. This striking colt has lightened legs, but not white, as in the sorrel mule.

cause chafing since the hide is not quite as hardy.

CHESTNUT: There is much confusion as to the difference between a chestnut and a sorrel mule. Let's get clear on this issue so we all can quit arguing! The chestnut is consistent, strong red all over the body and limbs of the mule, with minimal white.

Body color: Bright red or rust body color.

Mane and Tail: The mane and tail are the same color as the body.

Ears: Ear tips are the same as the body color, not black as in the bay mule.

Eye Area: Usually same as the body color; the eye area may have lighter to white circles.

Lower Nose: White or a lighter shade of body color in the nose.

Inner Legs and Underbelly: The inner legs and underbelly are either the body color or a lighter shade of the same. Some chestnuts have minimal white in the flanks and/or inner front legs, however this is not as prominent as in the sorrel mule.

Lower Legs: Same as body color; the lower legs of the chestnut may be a smidgen lighter nearing the hoof. Rarely do they have white lower legs.

Hooves: Black.

SORREL: The sorrel mule is again a reddish color, but not as red or as strong of coloring as the chestnut. The sorrel will have white points.

Body color: Red/orange diluting out to gold, blond, or even palomino coloring in the body.

Mane and Tail: The mane and tail of the sorrel will range from his body color and lighter to white and all shades in between.

Ears: The ears are the same as body color.

Photo courtesy of Shannon Garnaat, Liberty Hill Farm, Natural Dam, AR.

Wyatt from Liberty Hill Farm is a good representation of the sorrel mule. Wyatt models his white mane and lower legs.

Eye Area: The sorrel has more prominent white circles around his eyes than the chestnut.

Nose: The sorrel mule may also have a white blaze or stripe down his nose, with the lower nose being white in most cases.

Inner Legs and Underbelly: This mule usually possesses white on his underbelly and inside both his front and hind legs.

Lower Legs: Sorrels appear lighter to white in color from the knees and hocks down to the hooves.

Hooves: Hoof color depends on the lower legs. Most sorrels have white legs, and therefore their hooves are white. If the mule has darker, sorrel-colored legs, then black hooves would apply.

To simplify and clarify the difference between a sorrel and a chestnut mule, here is a general, yet pretty accurate, rule of thumb. If the bright red mule is the same strong color throughout most of his body, and his mother is a light horse breed, he can usually be identified as a chestnut mule. If the red/orange/blond mule has lots of white on him, especially close to the ground, and he is out of a draft horse mare, he can safely be called a sorrel mule.

Other Colors

We also have controversy over the durability of the remaining mule colors. Many breeders breed simply for color. This means their goal is for the offspring to possess bold and/or lively spots, as in the pinto/paint or appaloosa coloring. Below is the research of experts who have studied hair and hide, along with ones who have had extensive dealings with the mule, back in the time when the mule was their everyday partner and true beast of burden.

Ben Green in *The Color of Horses* speaks about the colored hide, which consists of spotted, paint/pinto, or appaloosa coloring.

> *...is much thinner and is subject to scalding, blistering and peeling. White hide around the eyes does not deflect sunlight and the eyes are more apt to be sore from the absorption of light. A dark eye enables better vision, especially at night.*
>
> *The dark hoof is stronger than the white and less apt to crack and split. The white foot does not hold the natural oils that normally prevent the hoof from cracking. The walls of a white hoof are soft and wear and break more easily from rough terrain than those of a dark colored hoof. The dark hoof seems to carry a shoe longer.*[14]

Below is an excerpt from Harvey Riley's book, *The Mule,* on his experience with the durability of colors in mules. Keep in mind, however, that the mule was used extensively and put to hard work in the late 1800s. Today, most mules are not put to the test so consistently as when this book was written.

> *In handling this large number of animals, I aimed to ascertain which was the best, the hardiest, and the most durable color for a mule. I did this because great importance has been attached by many to the color of these animals. But color is not a criterion to judge by.*
>
> *The mule that breeds closest after the jack, and is marked like him, is the hardiest, can stand fatigue the best, and is less liable to those diseases common to the horse; while those which breed close after the*

mare, and have no marks of the jack about them, are liable to all of them.

There is an exception to this, perhaps, in the cream colored mule. In most cases, these cream colored mules are apt to be soft, and they also lack strength. This is particularly so with those that take after the mare and have manes and tails of the same color. Those that take after the jack are more hardy and better animals. I have frequently seen men, in purchasing a lot of mules, select those of a certain color, fancying that they were the hardiest, and yet animals would be widely different in their working qualities.

It is very different with the white mule. He is generally soft, and can stand but little hardship. I refer particularly to those that have a white skin (as opposed to a gray mule with dark skin where the hairs have turned white with age.) Next to the white and cream, we have the iron grey mule. This color generally indicates a hardy mule.

In speaking of the color of mules, it must not be inferred that there are no mules that are all of a color that are not hardy and capable of endurance.

Avoid spotted or dappled mules; they are the very poorest animal you can get. They cannot stand hard work, and once they get diseased and begin to lose strength, there is no saving them. They generally have bad eyes, which get very sore during the heat and dust of summer, when many of them go blind. Many of the snow white mules are of the same description and about as useless. Mules with the white muzzle and with white rings around the eyes, are also of but little account as work mules. They can stand no hardship of any kind.

In purchasing mules, you must look well to the age, form, height, eyes, size of bone and muscle, and disposition; for these are of more importance than his color. Get these right and you will have a good animal.[15]

If one desired to complicate mule colors, it would be extremely easy to do. However, simplicity is the name of the game in mules, and it is my desire to keep it that way, even with identifying their color.

CHAPTER 7:
FITTING TACK—
DRESSING YOUR MULE

"DOES THIS SADDLE SHOP HAVE A MULE SECTION?"

With all the positive qualities mules possess, one frustrating obstacle owners inevitably have to face is that their mule is built slightly differently than a horse. This factor in itself is not a bad thing. What becomes frustrating is that most retail saddle and tack shops stock only horse equipment. Most mule folks have no choice other than to adapt horse-intended tack to their mule. In most cases this works just fine. But the mule does have a few special needs in the equipment he wears. Below are some things to be aware of in fitting your mule for his personal wardrobe.

Saddle

Fitting a horse saddle on the mule is the standard practice for most mule riders. There are custom-built mule saddles available today; some fit the mule just fine, while others fit the mule about the same as a horse saddle. The main difference in a mule saddle starts at the saddle tree, and most saddle trees are built for the horse, not the mule. When inquiring to a saddle maker about building a saddle for your mule, first ask for names and numbers of some of his customers who have had their mule saddles for six months or more. Call them up and ask them how they like their saddle and if they still are using it regularly. I add this because I find that some folks pay high prices for their custom-built mule saddle and don't seem to use

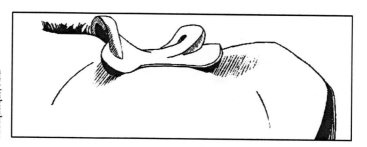

Illustration by Lori Mirmesdagh, Albuquerque, NM.

This is an incorrectly fitting saddle tree, upon which traditional western saddles are built. Note the gaps between tree and mule.

them after a while, returning to their horse saddles. Remember, the saddle not only has to feel good on top, where you sit, but also on the bottom, where it sits on the mule.

The mule walks and moves differently than a horse. And considering that some mules are virtually witherless, the saddle may have a tendency to slide forward on the mule. This is why you often see a breeching or crupper strap attached to the rear of saddles that are sitting on the backs of mules.

Jack McCloskey, a saddle maker from Canyon Country, California, has built many saddles to fit the mules that haul tourists up and down the steep trails of the Grand Canyon. Since 1978 he has studied saddle making and has found that there are two types of backs found on most mules: the lighter-sized mule, with a narrow back, and the rounder-barreled mule, with a flatter back. The rounder, larger mule is the toughest to squeeze into a horse saddle; therefore, most of McCloskey's custom-made saddles are built for the mule that has the relatively flat back and weighs over 1,000 pounds. In the following article, McCloskey explains:

"Mules have terrible backs for holding a saddle. A mule's back is different from a horse's back. They bulge at the rib cage from the cinch pocket, which also tends to help push the saddle forward. The horse has more withers and curve to its backbone, almost a natural saddle curve and a nice gentle flow off the back to the ribs. Mules are built somewhat backwards from a horse. The mule is more pointed toward the chest with a wider rib cage while the horse is heavier towards the chest with a smaller rib cage. The saddle tends to slip

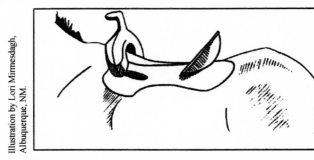

Illustration by Lori Mirmesdagh, Albuquerque, NM.

Here is a correctly fitting saddle tree. Note the conforming of the saddle
to the back of the mule for a flush fit.

*backwards on a horse while on a mule it tends to slip forwards because
of the difference in conformation.*

*"I think anatomically the mule is a very different animal from the
horse. The mule's withers and back actually work underneath the
saddle. There's a mass of muscle tied into the withers. When you
watch them walk, unsaddled, the whole withers move which is different
from a horse's back.*

*"The mule's withers need more space, more freedom than a horse
seems to need. The mule saddles I've designed sit back an inch to an
inch and a half further behind the withers as compared to a horse
saddle and it sits down, lower and flatter on the back. Now everything
seems simple, but it took many years to get to this point. It's not
perfect yet, but it's the closest I've ever seen to a good mule saddle.*

*"Almost all horse saddle trees are built so the bars flair out on all the
edges and there are built-up areas, round like a ball—these are what
cause the half-dollar sized scars on the mule's back. My saddle is
actually flat with a slight convex on the bars."*

*McCloskey uses trees made of wood that have a degree of give to them
such as spruce. Hard wood trees have no give and often crack under
great pressure, while the spruce gives to the pressure, lessening the
chances of the (saddle) trees being damaged. The spruce trees can
absorb shock better, such as in roping when a great deal of stress hits
the saddle all of a sudden. Hardwood saddle trees have been known to
snap under such circumstances. He said that plastic trees are also
affected more easily by weather and are more prone to be damaged by*

extreme cold than wooden trees. Another negative aspect of the plastic tree is that as it ages the plastic becomes more brittle.[16]

The smaller-sized mules (up to 950 pounds) may have a narrow barrel that allows for one of the narrow-treed saddles—such as the ones made in the early 1900s—to fit relatively comfortably, without too much sliding forward. If necessary, you may need to attach a crupper strap (a padded leather strap that fits under the tail) or a breeching (a series of straps that fit over the top of the croup and down around the mule's hind end) to the back of the saddle, making sure either attachment fits properly—not too tight, not too loose.

With activities that require the mule to stop and start quickly and travel uphill and downhill frequently, both a well-fitting breeching and breast collar are good ideas to keep the saddle from shifting on the mule's back, which may possibly create sores and sore backs.

The best way to tell if your saddle is fitting your mule properly is to ride just long and hard enough to make the animal's back sweat. Then remove the saddle and make note if you see small, dry spots on your mule's back, usually at the four corners where the saddle tree itself rides. This may be an indication that the saddle is too tight in these areas and may be causing discomfort to your mule.

If you do find dry spots, take three fingers and begin to press into the back of your mule at those areas. Does he move away, flinch, or sway his back to the pressure? How about more subtle signs of discomfort, such as a swish of his tail, throwing his head, or laying his ears back? If he reacts in any of these ways, your mule may be trying to tell you he is in pain in these areas. It's imperative to listen to your mule.

With even greater misfit, the mule hairs on these spots will deaden and soon turn white. Please realize that adding more pads under the saddle may not necessarily help the situation any more than it would help to add a second pair of socks to feet that are suffering from your ill-fitting shoes.

The best way to outfit your mule's back is with a saddle that doesn't slide or create any dry or white spots, set upon a half-inch, 100 percent wool pad. Real wool allows the mule's back to breathe. Most synthetic pads do not allow air to circulate under the saddle quite as well. When it comes to packing a mule, do some checking around for the best breathable pad available.

Bridle

There is very little to be concerned with in fitting a bridle onto your mule's head. Usually a horse bridle works just fine. Be aware that a mule has a thicker throat latch area and a slightly bigger head compared to the horse, yet most horse bridles (full-size, not Arab- or cob-size) are easily adjustable to accommodate a mule. It is not recommended to use a one-ear bridle, as the mule has a wider ear base than the horse and irritation to the mule ear is possible.

The bit should ride comfortably, with maybe a wrinkle in the mouth. Do note that the mule mouth is just a touch narrower than the horse mouth. Most average horse bits do fit the mule fine, however. The bit in the mule's mouth does not need to be any more severe than that of his cousin, the horse. If the mule has learned to give to the bit properly (which seems to take more time and patience than one expects), then a simple snaffle,

Photo courtesy of Mark Schrimpf, Bar S Performance, Krum, TX.

Chaparita models a standard horse bridle, which usually fits the mule just fine.

standard curb bit, or hackamore will suffice if your riding is in a ring. When taking your mule on the trail or out of a confined area, make sure he wears a bit with a short shank and curb chain, or a mechanical hackamore, especially if he is young and/or needs a little extra encouragement to stop when asked.

If a more severe bit seems to be needed, it is most beneficial to find where the problem stems from (usually in training the mule to tuck his head and give to the bit), instead of adding controlling and forceful devices. Severe bits, tie downs, martingales, and such equipment only signify that the handler has not taken the proper training time and patience to take care of a problem and is trying to "mask a deep cut with a small bandage."

Some horse bridles have a throat latch strap that is too small for the mule. Make sure the throat latch strap on the bridle you intend to use is plenty big enough. The purpose of the throat latch is simply to keep the bridle on the mule's head. Without a throat latch strap, it is possible, when riding in the brush, for a branch to slip under the headstall and slide the whole bridle off the mule's head, leaving the rider reins that go nowhere and do nothing!

This throat strap should never be tight or even snug. When a mule is working hard and breathing heavily, his windpipe expands considerably in his throat. The throat latch strap should never interfere in his breathing. If you ever have to decide between a snug throat latch strap or no strap, take the strap off the bridle to give your mule freedom of breath.

Harness

Most work harness of a saddle horse size (rather than one built for the draft horse) will fit a saddle mule. You will find that true old-style mule harness has a different type of blinder. This blinder is in the shape of a teardrop rather than a rectangle. The teardrop shaped blinder was originally designed for the mule. The collar should fit just as it does on the horse, with a three-finger gap at the base of the collar and a flat-hand gap in the side. Harvey Riley attended to many government mules in the late 1800s, and his experience spanned thirty years in the management of these mules. In his book, *The Mule*,[7] he stated about the harness:

> *If the animal does not work easy in it, if it (the collar) pinches him somewhere, let it (the collar) remain in water overnight, put it on the animal wet the next morning, and in a few minutes it will take the exact*

Photo courtesy of Katrina Walker, Wilson Creek Plowing Days, Wilson Creek, WA.

Harnesses vary in style. This four-up hitch wears the collar and hames work harness. Jog and light carts pull fine with the simpler breast collar harness.

formation of the animal's neck. There is an exact place for the bulge of the collar, and it is on the point of the mule's shoulder.

Breeching...see that it does not cut and chafe the animal so as to wear the hair off or injure the skin. If you get this too tight, it is impossible for the animal to stretch out and walk free. Besides obstructing the animal's gait, however, the straps will hold the collar and hames so tight to his shoulder as to make him sore on the top of his neck. These straps should always be slack enough to allow the mule perfect freedom when at his best walk.

In conclusion, just be aware of the fact that problems with your mule may stem from the clothes he wears, rather than a bad attitude. Be sure all his equipment fits properly. If you are not sure, find a person you trust to take a look at the equipment to see if your mule is fitting into his clothes correctly.

CHAPTER 8:
BUYING THE IDEAL MULE

"MY MULE IS BETTER THAN YOUR MULE."

There seems to be an ultimate that owners strive for in purchasing or breeding for their ideal mule. This vision can change frequently, depending upon the current fad and/or personal preference of the owner, breeder, or future buyer.

The laboring men of yesteryear quite often would take the rankest, ugliest mares they felt were not worthy of a stallion and breed them to any available jack, to produce a mule which provided them with tough, durable farm help. Most of these hardy offspring withstood the rigorous, intensive, slave-type work required of that era. As you can imagine, the result of this poorly planned cross also produced rank mules with as irregular conformations and dispositions as their mothers and fathers. The training methods for these inferior mules were just as crude as their lineage. This may be why the mule became known as a mean, stubborn, ugly animal. Today, it seems some uninformed folks still harbor thoughts of the mule as undesirable.

In the current age, the quality mare is bred with the best jack available. As today's equine enthusiasts know, the resulting mule has become a highly respected breed of animal with intelligence, beauty, versatility, and kindness. It is my desire to change the old reputation into the new with *all* folks. The next chapter will address breeding in order to produce that nearly perfect mule foal. This chapter deals with suggested guidelines to buying this worthy, ideal mule.

Questions to Ask Yourself

If buying the ideal mule is your goal, you must first ask yourself some very important questions. The right questions will eliminate many of the pitfalls that some people experience in purchasing their mule. The questions below are to help you clarify what you want in a mule, and will give you insight and clues on how, and if, a mule fits into your life. After that, you need to ask more questions to find out who this particular mule really is, and what problems he packs around, if any. After all these questions are answered, only then need you study the conformation points listed later to see if your chosen mule has your desired visual appeal.

Can you commit to having a mule?

We all know that getting any animal is not an easy decision. If you have dogs, cats, horses, bovines, or other animals, you already have committed to the responsibility of caring for them—in sickness and in health. You also have committed to providing suitable housing, a natural living environment, space to move around, and buddies to hang with if appropriate, plus adequate time and energy for that special attention and training.

Buying a mule requires the same commitment as any other animal, and sometimes more. A mule needs pasture and room to run around with free-choice shelter. He requires twice-a-day feeding when grass is not available for him to graze. This means you prepare for these times by putting up hay in your barn—a barn ideally large enough to hold several tons of hay. A mule needs fresh water available daily—even when the temperature is below freezing and all outside water is frozen solid. Your commitment to your mule may mean you find a clean bucket and haul fresh water from the house. A mule also requires your time and energy to work him frequently in his job (most mules prefer to have jobs). And finally, a mule needs to have company, which may mean obtaining another animal (more on this in Chapter 11, Mule Care).

What are you going to use your mule for?

Decide what you want to do with your mule. Most people want a good-looking mule that can perform a specific activity or two with expertise, who has a great attitude and minimal problems. If a winning conformation is most important to you, then delve heavily into the conformation points later

68

Pick a mule skilled in, or capable of, an activity that interests you. Sally and author practice tricks for a comedy show.

Photo courtesy of Michelle Dirkse, Seattle, WA.

in this chapter. Caution: a great show coloring or conformation doesn't do you much good in the long run if the mule's attitude is poor.

Determine what sport or activity interests you. Review Today's Mule as a Sport Animal in Chapter 2 if you're not sure what you would like to do with your mule. What activities catch your interest? Those activities are a good checklist to find what mule activity excites you. Fear or inexperience may be in the way today, but won't necessarily be tomorrow. If you really have a liking for dressage but think you would fail in any performance, don't switch courses and choose a mini mule just because he's cute. What if tomorrow you suddenly found courage and decided you wanted to pursue dressage? Your mini mule would be too small to be a ride-able dressage animal. Then where would you be?

Look for a mule out of a breed of horse that does a great job in your chosen skill. A pulling mule would best be out of a draft mare, a racing mule should be out of a thoroughbred mare, a good cow mule would be out of a quarter horse mare whose lineage excels in that sport. If you just want a pet and don't have much land, try a mini mule or two. If you want a practical, calm trail mule, it's not recommended to buy a mule out of a high-strung, hot-blooded horse. Common sense is the key, of course.

If you feel drawn to take on an abused mule to see if you can build trust again, bless your heart. Sorry to say, but there are plenty of those mules out there needing you to find them. This can be a lifelong, but very rewarding process. And I honor anyone willing to give of themselves for the betterment of helping an abused mule to finally have a good home.

Should I buy a foal or an older horse?

A number one important question to ask is, who needs the training, you or the mule? One of you must know what you are doing. What are your skills? Are you experienced and successful in handling mules? Are you experienced handling horses? Do you have any experience with donkeys?

If you need the training, by all means do not buy, or breed for, a young colt or filly. That youngster will certainly train you and have you running around in circles in no time—and not necessarily in a sane fashion! If you need mule experience, I suggest you begin your search for the trained mule, one who can teach you all about mules. Buy a foal only if you have the expertise in training, an abundance of time, and a desire to create a great mule. If you so desire to buy a young, untrained mule *after* you have been trained by a good mule, then by all means go for it.

Should I get a john mule or a molly mule?

This is a personal preference (see Sexuality and Fertility of the Mule, Chapter 5). A proper decision here is important. There are three possible answers:

- "I definitely want a john mule."
- "I definitely want a molly mule."
- "It definitely doesn't matter."

Where to Look

When you have answered the above questions, then you can begin your search for the ideal mule. There are several places where you may find this ideal mule. Let's address a few of these.

Auctions

This is a risky place to buy a mule. Usually you have no owner to ask questions and no way to get all the information you need to make an educated decision. Besides, you may only have a couple of hours or less to make the decision on this mule, which is no time to bring a vet out for a check-up or to contact a former owner.

Some mule problems are hidden. Auctions can be used by sellers to dump a mule that has problems, where the new buyer cannot bring the mule back when he learns of these problems. The current owner knows where the mule will fail, and he may not want the prospective buyers to find this information out.

On the other hand, I have had reports from many folks who have had great success buying a mule from an auction. It is a fast way to buy, usually cheaper than if you buy from a private party, plus you may be saving the life of a mule by purchasing him at an auction. If you trust your gut feelings and an auction mule "feels right," you may have just bought yourself a great animal!

Photo courtesy of Cindy Binning, Cindon Mules, Woodburn, IA.

The ideal mule is one who is safe for children—under supervision, of course. Sara monitors Cherokee, with son, Lane, aboard.

Private Parties, Breeders, Classified Ads

Most mules are sold and bought through these mediums. This gives you the opportunity to study the mule, try him out, thoroughly handle him, take time, and really evaluate him. If you find the seller has more than one mule for sale, find out why there is a price difference. Your mule may have a problem the owner is reluctant to tell you about, which is reflected in the lower price. Why is he selling the mule? This is an excellent question, especially if the seller has other mules that are not for sale. Remember, the most problematic get sold first!

When You Think You've Found Him

When you have found a great mule, then you can take a further step and begin to ask more questions and handle this particular mule. Usually mules do not have papers and your only information is what the owner tells you. Sometimes a potential sale overshadows truthfulness in sellers.

Mess with all parts of the mule body.

A good mule will handle most anything you do with him without much complaining. Ask the owner to pick up all four of his mule's feet, mess with his ears, and touch him all over. Watch how the mule handles it. Is he overly concerned, laying his ears back or swishing his tail? Watch if the owner is leery of doing these things and tiptoes cautiously around the mule. Be careful if the owner tells you that his mule is so gentle that even you could do these things and defers your request for him to handle his own mule by having you pick up his feet. However, some good mules are leery of new people and may not be willing to let you, a stranger, handle them at first. A mule can become attached to one person and not want others to mess with him. If the owner can get what he wants with ease and a willing response from the mule, you probably will be able to also. When it is just you and the mule, the mule will generally transfer his "one-person-itis" onto you once you earn his trust and respect.

If you feel comfortable handling this mule, pick up his foot, hold it, move it around, and pound on the bottom like you are nailing on a shoe. Pull his tail, rub his ears, and touch all of his body parts. Also, put pressure on his backbone and on the bars where the saddle rides to see if there is tenderness, which may indicate a possible injury or undue sensitivity (see Fitting Tack,

Chapter 7). In doing any and all of these things, watch his reactions closely. Does he lay his ears back, shiver his skin, and/or step away? He may be trying to tell you of pains in his body. To go even further, if you feel safe in doing so, perform these tasks with the mule being totally free and unrestrained to walk away, and see if the mule stands there and loves the handling or is somehow worried about his body—or you.

Ask the veterinarian.

Get the name and phone number of the vet who knows your prospective mule well. Ask him about the mule's health, past and present. What ailments have afflicted him and what resulting problems may occur because of it? Most mules are pretty healthy and may not have had too many dealings with the veterinarian. Ask the mule owner these questions also. If there were any medical problems that this mule experienced, then find the vet who treated him. If there is no known veterinarian, find one. Pay to have a trusted and/or the best qualified vet come out and look over your prospective mule. It will tell you how the mule feels about strangers, about vets, and of course about his health. Have the vet look at his teeth and tell you his age, if appropriate.

Ask the farrier.

Get the name and phone number of the farrier who knows this mule. Ask him about his feet activity in the past and present. Ask him about the trimming and shoeing behavior of the mule. If the owner has many different farriers in one locale, then it may be a problem to trim or shoe this mule. Ask him why he doesn't have a steady farrier. Good farriers usually are very busy and can pick and choose what animal they want to work with. If this mule presents a real trimming or shoeing problem, the farrier would just as soon spend his time on less problematic animals and may refuse to work on a troublesome mule.

Ask the trainer.

If the owner has sent the mule to a professional trainer, by all means contact that person. Find out every little detail you can so you will know what to expect from this mule. What are his idiosyncrasies? What does the mule know and where do his problems lie? Some problems may include catching, touching ears, saddling, bridling (taking the bit), giving to the bit, bucking, and attitude. Most all of these things can be part of a bad attitude or the result of an injury.

Ask the former owner.

Get the name and phone number of the former (as opposed to the current) owner of this mule. See if the mule was imprinted as a newborn foal (see Chapter 14, Solving Mule Problems). Usually the former owner has nothing to gain in hiding problems about the mule and is willing to help, unlike the current owner, who could lose a sale if he admitted the mule bucked occasionally under saddle.

Can I lease him first?

This is the best way to determine if you want this mule as your own. Taking the mule to your home and using him as you would if he was your own mule will quickly determine if he is worth purchasing for life. See if you can try out this mule on a one-year, six-month, three-month, or thirty-day trial period. Not only will this tell you if you both are right for each other, it also will tell you how he will get along with your other animals, or how he will be alone if there are no other animals present. Having a lone mule is not

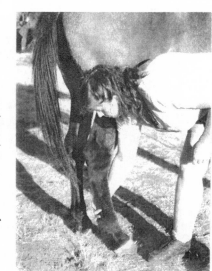

Photo courtesy of Michelle Dirkse, Seattle, WA.

Examine a prospective sale mule closely (when absolutely safe), as purchasing a mule is a commitment for life.

recommended (see "Mules Prefer Company" in Mule Gossip, Chapter 10).

There are many structured leases. There are leases with a price attached and ones that are on good faith as long as you take care of the mule, keep his feet trimmed, feed and worm him, and give him his necessary yearly shots. There are complete books strictly on leases and equine contracts that can be helpful if needed.

What tack did the former owner use?

This is an added question to give you some further insight on how the owner felt it was necessary to handle his mule. Pay attention to the tack used. Did he use a chain around the nose or under the chin when leading? These could be signs of an extremely headstrong mule or a lazy mule. What bit did he use—easy or severe? A severe bit may mean the mule has a lack of sensitivity to the bit or has never learned to tuck his head properly. Usually these things are the result of poor training; however, it can tell you where the mule is today and how much additional training he may need to become soft and responsive. Does the saddle have a breeching attached? Is there a breast collar hanging off the saddle on that saddle rack? You may have to add these items to properly outfit this particular mule.

Other thoughts and questions.

If you want to drive your mule, ask if he drives singly, if you expect to ever use him in this manner. Some mules do not like to pull alone and prefer working with a buddy. Ask if he drives in a multiple hitch, and where he is positioned within that hitch. Has the owner ever switched the mule's hitch position? How does he perform in another hitch spot? What if you purchased two separate mules and both wanted to be hitched on the left side, not cooperating fully when hitched on the right? Unless you are set up for tandem pulling or a four-up hitch, this may be a problem!

If you want to pack your mule, ask if he has ever packed before. If he has, ask if he ever packed fresh meat on his back. Some mules are squeamish and *do not* want to carry a dead elk. A very well-trained pack mule has no problem with hauling meat. The last thing you want when you are hunting and miles from nowhere is to find out that the animal you just killed cannot be hauled out because you can't get it near the mule! If you want to hunt with your mule, ask if he has ever had a rider shoot a rifle while mounted.

This takes extra training and is bonus points for a prospective owner, if this will be a useful skill.

Conformation

After the above questions are answered to your satisfaction, you can then delve into the visual aspect of your ideal mule. The more closely the mule follows the ideal horse conformation standards, the more visually attractive the mule is to most people. Picture in your mind the wide variety of horse breeds—from the refined bone of the high-strung Thoroughbred to the stockier, more sensible Quarter Horse, to the coarse bone structure and docility of the Belgian draft horse. Then realize that mules come from just about any breed of the horse, and therefore they come in all shapes, sizes, and temperaments. Two mules may look entirely different, yet both are well-conformed animals. The differences are simply individual breed type rather than conformation faults.

Even if you are an amateur mule enthusiast, you still can evaluate mule conformation just by analyzing what you see through your own eyes. Do the body parts flow into each other? There should not be any one body part that attracts undue questionable attention. Your overall study of the ideal mule from top to bottom should be pleasing, smooth, and balanced. The closer and more frequently you examine mules, the better your eye becomes at judging the overall picture.

Attitude

The one consistent desirable mule characteristic that never goes out of fashion is attitude. Before body conformation is reviewed, most important to the value of a mule is his temperament. A great assessment of the mule attitude can be revealed by looking into his eyes. The ideal mule has a "kind eye" which shows docility, playfulness, trust, and overall kindness.

The less-than-ideal mule could present an eye of unjust fear and evil that may be the result of an attitude problem. Believe me, it isn't easy to change the attitude of a mule! Above all, your ideal mule will be one you like as a fellow critter. This will provide that unique mule personality that is irresistible to the human!

The more stories I get about rank mules, the more I learn that many bad mule attitudes stem from injuries. Some of these poor critters are not people-haters, but may simply be in constant pain. Regularly, I receive stories from folks that have the heart to take in these "deemed useless" animals and then learn their mule has been hurting from an injury all along and his trust in people is very low. When measures are taken to bring the mule out of pain and to restore trust, after a while these useless long-eared throw-aways quite frequently become man's best friend and partner.

Head, Neck, Withers

The ears of the ideal mule are long, actively alert, and clean cut. The throat latch area will be clean, in that it does not wrinkle each time the mule tucks his head. The head will be proportionate to the body, not overly big or coarse, and definitely lacking a Roman nose. Some people appreciate a mule with the head of a donkey, deeper-set eyes, and a protruding eyebrow bone. Others prefer a mule head with the refinement of a horse's head. Again, this is debatable only to the personal preference of the individual mule enthusiast.

Photo courtesy of Mary Ann Wentworth, Earlham, IA.

Mary Ann Wentworth riding Snickers, a very well-put-together mule with an alert, willing attitude.

The ideal mule neck will have length and flexibility and will blend into the shoulder and withers—which will be prominent enough to hold a saddle in place. Most mules have low withers and the saddle may slip on their backs. A mule can carry a short, thick neck, which will not hinder the flexibility of an animal which is naturally bullheaded and strong-necked, anyway.

Body, Legs, Chest

A mule's back is different from a horse's back. You will find one of two styles of mule backs. Both are fine body styles. The mule weighing in up to 900 pounds usually has a narrower back, dropping from the backbone. These mules can usually carry a narrow pommel, high-backed saddle with little difficulty. The bigger mule may have an overly flat back and be more on the "roly-poly" size (see Fitting Tack, Chapter 7). This again is the personal preference of the owner, as both styles can be ideal.

The ideal back will not be overly long, as this can cause a weakness if the mule is intended to carry heavy packs or oversized humans. The rump will be as round and full as possible. The rear of the mule usually drops from the croup like a donkey rump, and is not as full as that of the horse. This has no detriment to the mule's working ability, only to the overall look of the mule. The tail of the ideal mule will originate outside the body, not inset in the buttocks.

The legs of the ideal mule will flow out of the shoulders and hindquarters, whittling down to solid cannon bones and tough hooves. The chest is plenty wide enough so that it does not look like his front legs originate from one hole instead of two when viewed straight on.

Indeed, the mule is weakest where the horse is strongest. The muscles and tendons of mules' small legs are not capable of carrying an overly heavy body weight for any length of time. It stands to reason if you feed him until he gets two or three hundred pounds of extra flesh on him, as many owners do, he may break down for lack of leg-strength.

Viewing from the rear, the hocks of the ideal mule are straight, and all four hooves point forward. In many cases, you see a horse's body held up by cow-hocked donkey legs and turned-out hooves. Again, this is usually no detriment to the travel or working ability, only to the visual aspect.

Action

The mule's athletic performance will be able to parallel that of the horse, and with the addition of his increased flexibility and intelligence, the mule will excel in some (if not most) cases. The ideal mule has a willing, smooth action that is somewhat horse-like, rather than the resistant donkey-like trot. Getting on his back and riding is the best way to judge a prospective mule and his gait.

The shoulder of the mule is generally more upright than the horse's, as the mule has a hip action that is slightly different. This trait, inherited from the donkey, produces movement of a forward and backward motion that is smoother and involves less side-to-side rocking than is common to the horse. To the layman, this means that when you ride a horse your body rocks side to side, and when you ride a mule your body rocks forward and back!

So, the bottom line in buying your ideal mule, is knowing what you want, where to find him, what to look for, and which questions to ask when you think you have found him. Then notice his kind attitude and pleasing conformation. Most of all, determine if this is the mule you want to live with for many years. Oh yes, one more thing—*good luck!*

CHAPTER 9:
CHOOSING JACKS AND MARES FOR BREEDING

"I'LL TAKE THIS APPLE AND THAT ORANGE."

If you feel you are qualified to raise a mule foal, this chapter will help to educate you to find an appropriate sire and dam to produce your own ideal mule.

If you could experience the perfect mule, you then may have a solid recipe to follow in your breeding program. Please note that there are *no* perfect animals. Imperfect mare and imperfect jack beget an imperfect mule, that's just the way it goes!

Breeding for mules can be a guessing game, as the same parents can produce different animals from one year to another. I have trained full brother mules that have similar conformation, yet completely opposite temperaments. One mule thought very donkey-like and reacted primarily through his fight instinct, having to temper his kicking desire. The other mule thought very horse-like and reacted out of fear, wanting to run away at any new situation or noise.

There are certain characteristics a potential breeder or owner should pay particular attention to when choosing a mare and a jack for the procreation of a mule. In a way, humans are attempting to mate apples and oranges. It therefore is extremely important to invest in making an educated decision about the sire and the dam to produce a sound, attractive mule with a great disposition, who will work with you in the capacity that you have chosen for years to come.

Good mules are hard to come by. Please don't just breed the worst mare you have because nobody can ride her. Instead, decide what activity you would like to use your mule for (see Today's Mule as a Sport Animal, Chapter 2) and then breed an appropriate mare and jack for that purpose. Below you will find considerations to look for in both the mare and the jack with your ultimate goal of reproducing your ideal mule.

Imprinting at birth is essential in producing a great mule. This timely activity shortly after birth alleviates what could be a barrel-full of problems later on in the mule's life. Please refer to Chapter 13, Training, and Suggested Readings at the end of this book for more information on imprinting a foal.

Jack Considerations

The donkey jack is used for two purposes: first, by serving the jennet to reproduce their own kind, and second, by serving a mare to produce a mule. Jacks perform better and more willingly when one that is intended to serve mares is used only on mares and one intended to serve jennets is used only on jennets.

When buying a jack, make sure he will cover mares if you intend on live breeding. Jacks that have been kept with or bred to jennets may refuse to breed horse mares, and jacks that have covered exclusively mares may not breed to jennets. An alternative solution to these challenges is to delve into the vast realm of Artificial Insemination (AI) and shipping semen to buyers who artificially inseminate whichever animal they choose with it.

The main rule of thumb in breeding for mules is to look at the offspring by either or both parents that have already hit the ground. This is the most effective means of telling you what the jack will throw as far as attitude, conformation, and action. Don't let geography get in the way of your jack choice. If you find a top-quality jack but he is thousands of miles away, it may be possible the owner can collect and ship semen from this jack to be artificially inseminated into your mare.

Photo courtesy of Westmar Mules, LLC, Kalispell, MT.

Mammoth jacks are popular for breeding with draft horse mares to produce the much desired draft mule. Westmar's Murel represents a fine looking jack for breeding.

Qualities Given to the Mule

The jack gives the mule his long ears, distinct bray, high intelligence, great endurance, sure-footedness, ability to endure heat and cold, strength, and instinctive sense of self-preservation. A good jack is characterized by a lack of complete influence. That is, he fails to impart all of his qualities to his mule offspring. The mare, more than the jack, strongly influences the height, body conformation, and general disposition of the mule.

Attitude

The most important aspect in breeding is to make sure the mule starts off with a genetically great attitude. Above all, make sure the mare and the jack both have good temperaments before you breed them together to create your ideal mule. The environment in which a mule foal is raised has a tremendous effect on his personality and character in later years. The mare needs to possess a docile temperament, aside from game-playing and obvious distrust in humans. A horse that you can handle in most any form without too much complaint is ideal. If the mare is cared for, loved, and disciplined, you can be pretty sure that the mule she produces will start off with a good attitude.

Look for docility in the jack. If you don't know the jack personally, pay particular attention to how the owner acts around him. Does he go into the field with him or just show him from outside the fence line or in a controlled environment? If he does enter the field with the jack loose, note if he is afraid of the jack and is moving cautiously around him like he may get kicked, bitten, or attacked at any moment. The best jack is one that is gentle, trained, and ridden instead of merely used for breeding. Trained jacks will generally have the best attitudes. Besides, you can hop on and learn the smoothness or roughness of this jack's gait, which is an indication of how his offspring will travel.

Most importantly, look at the attitude of the jack's previous mule children. Again, note the concerns and behaviors of the mule's owner when he presents this mule. The donkey jack is an intelligent animal. If you combine this intelligence with a rank disposition, you may create a cunning and possibly dangerous mule.

Head and Neck

The donkey can have a coarse, bony head with protruding brow bones, or you can find a donkey that has a clean, finer-bone type head with a straight profile. Again, it is personal preference in what type of head you want on your mule. Common sense comes into play also. Just remember that the large, coarse head of the donkey set upon the neck of a refined, smaller-boned mare may not be the best combination. The eyes of the jack and mare should be large, intelligent, and kind. The jack's ears should be clean cut, carried alert, and as long as possible.

Please stay away from breeding those ewe-necked mares for mules. Upon observation of the mule at a free trot, one distinct feature is his nose high in the air. The muscles in his lower neck seem to be more developed because of this action. This relates to the difficulty of teaching the mule to give to the bit and tuck his head properly. In this respect, breeding to a ewe-necked mare may enhance this undesired aspect. Both parents should possess a long neck, with the throat latch open and clean. Be careful that your mare doesn't carry a roman nose, as the mule already has a tendency for this type of nose.

Body

In choosing a mare for breeding, look for a round rump, high withers, and straight legs. The body of both parents should be deep and wide. Extra-long backs in the jack can produce a mule with a long and possibly weaker top line. The jack should have a fairly level croup. A goose rump in the mare is out. The mare should outweigh the mule she is to raise by about 150 pounds.

The jack's shoulder will usually be straight, but the more sloping the better. In the mare, the withers should be prominent and run as far back as possible. Make sure the mare possesses a wide chest and full body.

Legs and Height

The ideal mammoth jack has heavy bone and large, thick joints, with strong,

The right mare and jack can produce an ideal mule, if you have done your homework and planned ahead.

straight legs. A large-boned jack is to be preferred over one with finer bone, if all else is equal. The feet should be as large as possible in proportion to the animal since donkey hooves are smaller than those of the horse, and the mule is usually more of horse-size than donkey-size. Height is a personal human choice, as is true in the horse world. However, taller seems to be more desirable for the resale of the saddle mule, especially to carry large men. In breeding for a riding animal, it is wise to try to create a 15-plus hand mule. In packing, a good 14- to 15-hand mule is much easier for the packer to load than the taller ones and can handle weight nearly as well.

A 14.2-hand mare and a 14-hand jack can have up to a 15.1-hand mule. A mule colt will usually mature taller than the mare; how much taller is determined by the jack size.

Harness mules that are used in the fields are usually out of draft mares and are therefore taller, bulkier, and bigger boned. The height on a work mule is again a personal choice, although I would recommend choosing your team of relatively the same height and weight so they can work together best.

Hardy, functional, pleasant mules are by far the ideal to own. Here is expert advice from Harvey Riley's *The Mule*. Riley's job was to attend to many government mules in the late 1800s, and his experience spanned thirty years in the management of these mules.

> *The average sized, compact mare is by all odds the superior animal to breed mules from. Very large mules are about as useless for army service as very large men are for troopers. You can get no great amount of service out of either. One is good at destroying rations; the other at lowering haystacks and corn bins. The heavier you can get the bone and feet, the better. You can rarely get even this; the mule in nineteen cases out of twenty, breeds close after the jack, more especially in the feet and legs. It makes little difference how you cross mares and jacks, the result is almost certain to be a horse's body, a jack's legs and feet, a jack's ears and in most cases, a jack's marks. Nature has directed this crossing for the best, since the closer the mare breeds after the jack the better the mule. The highest marked mules, and the deepest of the different colors, I have invariably found to be the best, ...breeding from sound, serviceable, compact and spirited mares. You must in fact, use the same judgment in crossing these animals as you would if you wanted to produce a good race or trotting horse.* [7]

Photo courtesy of Marsha Smith, Mountain Fox Trotters, Coarsegold, CA.

Breeding for color in a mule is quite a challenge. The coloring on this mule is a rare gift to the owner. However, don't forsake attitude just to try and get flashy color.

Breeding for Color

In breeding for color, again, please do not overlook attitude and quality for the sake of spots. Color is difficult to attain in mules for some unknown reason. Below are some breeding guidelines according to donkey expert Betsy Hutchins, president of the American Donkey and Mule Society.

Black jacks often throw (black or) dark colts which are easy to match. Red (or roan) jacks are more likely to sire sorrel or lighter colored colts, especially from sorrel mares. Gray jacks sometimes sire light colored colts, and often the colt follows the color of the mother when the sire is gray.

A spotted jack (with a history of spots in his breeding on his sire's side) gives good service in breeding for pinto, white, or appaloosa mules. However, a good jack is worth a great deal to the breeder and color should be of his last consideration.[17]

ADVANCED SECTION:

ESSENTIAL MULE WISDOM

CHAPTER 10: MULE GOSSIP: TRUTH OR MYTH?

"DOES A MULE REALLY EAT LESS THAN A HORSE?"

In the quest for valuable mule knowledge, one will hear—or read—repeated blanket phrases. These statements are more like gossip when describing the mule, since such statements can do a great deal of injury. This gossip may discourage you in forming an honest picture and also may encourage you to improperly care for your mule. The extreme is that this could possibly lead to abuse through lack of information. In the following pages you will find some of the most repeated comments about the mule and the expanded truths behind them.

Work

Below is an assortment of frequently heard gossip comments concerning the working mule. If you were to assume these statements are completely true, you could easily overwork a mule—even with the best of intentions. There is some truth to these statements; however, you must view the big picture and then use the truth in its proper context.

The mule is stronger than the horse.

Keep in mind that the mule is usually a little bit smaller in overall size than the horse; and yes, pound for pound, the mule can endure slightly more weight. Absolutely do not use this as gospel, but judge each individual mule on his own physical ability. Don't just load him up heavier than you would a horse. Remember, you must work him up to a heavy load, just as you would work up to lifting heavier and heavier weights on your personal workout program.

Overpack a mule and he will buck off the load or lie down.

True, but you are smarter than that. You know to not load so heavily that your mule feels inclined to react this way.

A mule won't kill himself working.

True. They do have mule sense enough to stop when overly fatigued; however, use your human sense and do not work them to such an extreme.

Most are willing workers.

True, especially if you have a good rapport with your mule. However, if your mule has been handled incorrectly, he may be prone to laziness and/or defiance.

Physically tougher than the horse.

True. The mule has a steady way of going which allows him to endure longer, more consistent work. Some horses have an abundance of energy at the onset, but that energy can burn out quickly.

A mule won't intentionally harm himself.

This refers to the fact that the flight instinct does not take over as strongly as it does in the horse. When a horse gets in a tangled situation, such as wrapping his legs around barbed wire, it could be extremely dangerous to him. Most horses have a tendency to react with panic and try to fight their way out. A mule will usually not let that fear take over. He can switch over to a logic mode and figure out a solution rather than immediately reacting in fear.

Mules can tell time.

This refers to a mule that is on a regular work schedule. If you are working your mules daily and stop for a break at a consistent time, more than likely your mules will soon take it upon themselves to stop for a coffee break at that same time, with or without your request or even your permission!

Photo courtesy of Marsha Arthur, Yerington, NV. Photo of Jim Porter, Spring Canyon Mule Makers, Onyx, CA.

Precision and strength are needed for pulling logs out of the forest, *and* in arena competitions.

On the positive side of mules telling time, you can use this to your advantage. If your first chore in the morning is to feed your mule, you can be assured that you will never oversleep. His internal clock will go off at that particular hour; and his braying can be used for your morning alarm clock!

Mules can stand the heat and cold better than the horse.

True. Cowboys in Brazil and other South American countries prefer a mule over a horse because it handles the heat better. Plantation owners in the south choose mules over horses for their ability to stand up under intense heat and a long season. If the weather is unbearably hot, the mule slows his pace and no amount of prodding will hurry him. Here is a story (author unknown) that depicts the difference in heat tolerance between the horse and the mule.

It was a double show in Texas on a hot day. The palomino horses were in one arena and mules in another. They were all performing in the same classes, except that individual mules would participate in many classes—western pleasure, barrels, single driving, coon jumping, halter and probably an egg and spoon race along with a pole bending class—whereas the horses were more specialized and usually participated in only one or two classes.

After a time in the heat, the palominos were absolutely black with sweat. Upon purposely examining most of the mules, they were only sweating under their brow bands and saddle pads. The mules at that show drank one bucket of water each during the full day of seven classes. You also didn't see any mule owner hot walking his animal— except in rare cases such as endurance riding. Instead, most mules were turned loose to roll in the sand and cool themselves out.

This heat tolerance derives from the donkey, whose ancestry comes from the desert (see Idiosyncrasies, Chapter 12). The reason for their exceptional cold tolerance is yet to be understood.

Smarts

The mule is a highly intelligent animal. He figures things out quickly and is often one step ahead of his handler. Lack of information on how the mule thinks can be a detriment to the handler, the end result being frustration for both parties.

Mules are stubborn.

"Stubborn" is one of those words that mule people do not like to associate with their beloved companion, as it has negative connotations. The truth or myth of this statement depends upon your definition of stubborn. If stubborn means the mule will refuse to give in to every whim of the handler, then yes, they are stubborn, smartly stubborn. However, if stubborn means they will not work for a handler no matter what the circumstances, then I would have to say definitely *not*. The mule can be trying at times, and most stubbornness derives from the handler's inability to understand why his smart mule is resisting cooperation.

More intelligent than the horse.

True. As with all highly intelligent minds, the mule brain needs to be kept active and challenged. This is especially true with a young mule. He is a quick learner, and when bored, he can cleverly figure out obstacles such as gate latches and barn doors, and may even be difficult to keep inside a fence. Whatever he can conjure up to get into, such as taking bits of teachings and playing games with the handler's mind, he may do so—and enjoy the challenge! You should be prepared for this and figure out ways your mule can be adequately challenged in positive ways.

What do you do with a rank mule? Here's one job for him, the rodeo!

To illustrate their intelligence, here is one soldier's recollection. Robert Ivan Miller was assigned to the provisional remount in World War II. This unit was to supply the combat divisions with mules.

> *...Once an English officer and I were sent to Sardinia to bring back several hundred mules, which had belonged to the Italian Army. We were also to bring along Italian soldiers who had been trained as packers, and had worked with the mules. When we had our soldiers and mules assembled, a Liberty Ship was sent to us to transport them over to Italy. The mules were to be loaded aboard ship with a regular cargo net. The net would be placed on the dock, a mule led into it, and would be hoisted up to the deck of the ship. The mules, although the experience for them was a new and strange situation, remained calm and relaxed. We never had a single mule injured in the entire operation. I had purchased a fine horse on the island with my own funds for my personal use. He was to be the last animal loaded, but when led onto the net, he became very excited. When the hoist started to lift him, he began to paw and kick and finally fell out of the net when he was about 20 feet up in the air. He was so badly injured that I had to shoot him. Two attempts were made later to load horses by this*

*method and both failed. These incidents demonstrate that the mule has
more intelligence than the horse as well as stronger survival instincts.* [18]

Think for themselves in an emergency.

True. In a pinch, mules will rely on their own instinctual reasoning rather
than trust their handler's judgment. They have intuitively learned to take
care of themselves and know what is best for them.

Memory like an elephant.

Mules simply have to be second in line for this title! When the mule
experiences pain or fear, it takes a very long time and many repetitions of a
similar event without pain/fear for him to overcome one traumatic incident.
For example, a mule may not allow an unsuspecting new handler to pick up
his hind feet simply because years ago a farrier lifted his young rear leg up
too high and the mule nearly fell over, scaring himself to death.

Training

Can kick when provoked.

True. Do not provoke.

The mule is headstrong.

True. It is natural for a mule to be physically heavy and pushy with his head
and also emotionally pushy; he certainly wants things to go his way!

Will be persistent and wait until you give up/

True. You had better have an abundance of patience and plan on spending
all day working with a mule if necessary. Time and persistence will win out
for whoever has the most of both.

Can tell the difference between just and unjust punishment.

True. They know you better than you know yourself. You cannot fool a
mule by pretending to be nice when deep inside you are harboring anger,
fear, or prejudice. A handler who loves and respects mules will achieve
much more than a handler who merely tolerates them.

Companionship

Mules prefer company.

True. Just as we humans prefer to reside with another, the mule prefers to have his buddy nearby. The mule is a naturally dependent creature, and because of this, he can make very good friends with man, horses, mules, donkeys, goats, and other critters. Most often he does not do nearly as well if left alone in a field—out of contact with other critters—for an extended period, such as weeks, months, or years. If he cannot attach himself to another mule, a horse, or a donkey, he may settle for small livestock or a dog if available (see Idiosyncrasies, Chapter 12).

The young mule also needs to learn that he can be left alone and still be okay. Be sure to practice taking his buddy away at times, as a totally dependent mule can be a disaster to handle. The best way to pasture your young mule is to change his field mate(s) periodically, while keeping him in contact across the fence line. Independence in a mule is a very desirable characteristic, and if started young and maintained, a mule can learn to accept and enjoy change and independence.

Photo courtesy of Mary Bloodsworth, 3JM, Bonham, TX.

Mules do best with a buddy, as they are social animals. Here Fran and Blue are collaborating on *something!*

94

Herds of mules can be kept in small quarters without injuries.

True. Mules do not like pain and will not intentionally harm themselves. With their friendly nature, they generally will not harm any animal they are familiar with. When they fight amongst themselves, it is relatively mild compared to horses in the same situation. The mule's kick may simply be an attempt to gently push another mule away using his hind leg.

Mules like horses better than donkeys.

True. It seems that most mules will bond with a horse sooner than a donkey. The reason for this is probably because the mule's mother is a horse. That is not to say that the chosen horse will in turn bond to the mule as strongly!

Mules like people.

True. They are extremely friendly, and if they have experienced equality from humans, they can be your best friend—bordering on being a pest! If they have experienced human dominance and control, quite naturally they would probably rather not be around you.

Sense of humor.

True. Mules certainly are able and willing to play! The mule understands more than people know.

Care

Taking care of the mule is a sensitive subject. Please read Mule Care in Chapter 11 for the complete picture. Overall, the mule deserves the best of care, which means a natural living situation, ample food, clean and fresh water, and in and out shelter, combined with proper health and preventative measures to ensure a happy, healthy mule.

A mule will never overeat.

False. "Never" is a strong word. This is one of those blanket statements where you can really find yourself in trouble if you don't add some common sense. Yes, the mule has an innate sense of knowing when to stop eating, and on most occasions, he will eat until full and leave the rest, but there have been cases of colic and founder in mules. Don't just open the barn door and let him help himself without supervision. The best recommendation is to treat him like a horse until you are sure you know your mule.

Mules don't drink as much water.

When overheated, the mule will not usually require the monitoring of cold water consumption that is necessary for a horse, since he is not as prone to water founder. Young ones, however, may drink more water on an everyday basis than expected. Again, *know your mule.*

Also, do not be alarmed when you take your mule somewhere and he won't drink the water. Mules prefer clean, fresh, familiar-tasting water. If he cannot have that or the water at home that he is used to, he may not drink right away. After a day or so, he will adjust to what you give him, as long as it is good, clean water.

Eats uphill.

Of course he will have his front higher than his rear on a slope. Why would he point himself downhill, stretch his neck, and be uncomfortable when dining?

Can forage for food better than the horse.

True. He seems to like leaves and brush more than a horse does. Mules can be extremely picky eaters, though, and confusing at that. My molly will sometimes not eat sweet COB (a desirable grain made from corn, oats, and barley with molasses), but she will eat bad hay if I use it for her bedding!

Eats slower than a horse.

True. Your mule will eat slower than a horse and need that special time consideration when feeding together with his horse brothers. Make sure he has the proper quantity of feed, time, and space to eat it all.

Poop in certain areas.

In a field, the mule will have several mule-made manure piles. In a stall, he will find a favorite spot to poop, just like a horse stallion.

Medical

Please note that I am not a veterinarian. The most vet work that I have done is preventative maintenance, worming, and shots, along with occasional professional instruction in the healing of injuries. Please contact your veterinarian for professional assistance if there is *any* question about the health of your mule. See Mule Care in Chapter 11 for more on mule medical practices.

The mule has far fewer medical ailments compared to the horse.

True. The mule is definitely hardier and is not as prone to the wide array of horse problems. He may suffer lameness, colic, cold, and disease, but some of the advanced horse ailments seem to bypass the mule.

Mules can't colic.

False. The mule has been known to colic, although it is not as common as one will find with the horse. Again, preventative measures are encouraged.

Let Those Mule Folks Talk!

People love to tell mule stories. Some are a bit unbelievable, some seem very credible, some are sad, some are fascinating, and some are very informative. I have picked out some statements regarding training and understanding of the mule to give you more rounded mule wisdom.

> "The young unbroken mule cannot be made to understand what you are whipping him for. You may hitch him up today for the first time, and he may become sullen and refuse to go a step for you. This may be very provoking and perhaps excite your temper but do not let it, for ten chances to one, if you take him out of the harness today and put him in again tomorrow he will go right off and do anything you want. It is always best to get a young mule used to the harness before you try to work him in a team. When you get him so that he is not afraid of the harness (and noise), you may consider your mule to be two thirds broke...There is not a driver living who can rein them with the same safety that he can a horse...They do not lose all their senses when they get frightened and run away as a horse does. Bring a mule back after he has run away and in most cases he will not want to do it again. A horse that has once run away, however, is never safe afterward. I have

Photo courtesy of Cindy Binning, Cindon Mules, Woodburn, IA. Lane mounting Cherokee, with Sara and Scott Whirrett, and Don Parmer.

Most mule folks *love* their mules and want to share mule stories, even when others may need immediate assistance!

never found a habitual (mule) runaway. Their sluggish nature does not incline them to such tricks."[19]

"Loud, boisterous handlers tend to alienate the mule, while gentle but firm handlers seem to get more from him in riding, packing, driving and pulling. Mules have a tendency to run away while pulling. Until this habit is cured through daily use, the mule is not broke. This runaway trait is due more to fear than anything else so, the more gentle and easy to handle the animal is, the better your chances of controlling him in a tight situation." ("The Hybrid's Symmetrical Disposition," by Walt Rickell. The Brayer. *Issue unknown.)*

"If a mule balks, chances are it's your fault. Some little part of his world has fallen into disrepair, and it's up to you to fix it. If you must hit him, hit him in the act of disobedience, and never on the head. A mule distinguishes between just and cruel punishment, and will carry a grudge against a cruel man for as long as it takes to get even...Training takes a firm hand, long hours, and gumption. Never give up. Nothing worse than a half-broke mule. Keep them off heavy work such as breaking ground until they're five, and you'll have willing

help...Mules love order, so develop a working routine." *("Working Mules," by Thomas Ireland.* Western Horseman. *October 1980.)*

"Mules will separate the men from the boys. Crude and quick techniques that often work on horses won't always work on mules. If mules force us to use more patient and scientific horsemanship and fewer gimmicks, then I am all for them. Physically and psychologically, what we learn from mules will, I hope, benefit horses." (Lynn Miller. Small Farmers Journal.*)*

"Perhaps because of their cautious nature, to fully train a mule takes twice as long as a horse. Even when mules are well broken, they often won't let a stranger ride or handle them." (Larry McKim, DVM, from Glendale, Arizona)

The following are additional words of wisdom. These authors are unknown.

"One theory pertaining to training is that a horse has a stronger fear instinct which prevents him from learning as quickly since in most cases you have to get through the fear before any real learning takes place."

"You have to be smarter than the mule, which means you have to know how his mind works to stay one step ahead of him."

"A well trained team of mules can teach you more than any man, if you are patient and attentive to their ways."

"Donkeys are noted for mannerisms that may make them refuse to do something until they are absolutely positive that you are going to make them do it. Then they give right in and cooperate like angels. Don't use strength with a mule, either out-think him or use physical means to calmly outmaneuver him. Call your mules bluff. Once you do that you have won. The key to handling mules is do things simply, calmly, and firmly. The big secret to calm mules that never kick and don't have bad habits is handling them firmly but gently from the time they are born or from the time you acquire them. When a mule resents something and resists, from then on you can expect a fight. You must be especially persistent. You must quietly ease a mule through all of the initial steps of training until he accepts it. Then you'll have no trouble."

"If you want him to work too hard for his own well being, especially in hot weather, if you want him to cross that rickety wooden bridge with no proof that it will be safe, if you try to frighten or hurt him to make

him cross he will definitely be stubborn and may even fight back, and a mule can aim a kick for best results."

"Don't buy one of a team of mules and expect any good work. Except for the occasional, very independent, individual mules, most mules need a teammate. If they don't have one, they can't concentrate on their work and may be totally useless. They will also have inseparable friends in their pasture. Train them early to leave their friends no matter how rough it is. Older mules get along better if they have been carefully handled in this respect when young. Young mules are rather insecure animals and the natural herd instinct is exceptionally strong in them because of this. The favorite pal of any mule is a horse, probably because his mother was a horse."

"When training is interrupted, a mule retains its past instruction and can be retrained from the point where it was discontinued. Experienced mule people believe the animal is so attuned to its surroundings that it can sense its handler's mood even as he approaches."

"Once mules are acquainted with their handler, their performance is quite predictable. They seldom get nervous enough to prance or refuse to walk in the show ring. Indeed, almost any mule team will make a good show with no warm-up, if necessary. Because of this fact, it is important to break them out well without serious problems, because early training is remembered a lifetime."

"If you are going to do something with a mule, you need to go ahead and do it with authority. If you hesitate or back off when a mule lays its ears back and lifts a hind leg, you will not get the job done. A mean mule can be very mean."

"If a mule runs away it won't hurt itself...so you won't get hurt (if you are riding the mule). It won't run into fences and trees like a horse will, and they won't go into an area that they instinctively know is dangerous."

"It will seldom attempt to jump an object or go anywhere unless it is certain of making it safely. What some call stubbornness is the mule's meticulous concern for his own health; he will not overwork. If you ask him to go where he does not feel safe, be prepared for a fight."

"Handled properly they learn to like people and are easy to catch. That's important in the hills as it is their tendency to quickly become attached to the animals they run with. You can picket your saddle horse with your mules loose and get a good night's sleep knowing that your mules will be there in the morning."

"Teach the lesson thoroughly. Once the lesson is taught, repeat it occasionally to enforce it. When he gets bored, stop...The mule enjoys taking bits and pieces of the teaching and play games with the handler's mind."

CHAPTER *11: MULE CARE*

"HOW CAN I BEST TAKE CARE OF MY MULE?"

We all want to take care of our mule in the best way possible. If we just knew what that was! I believe the most effective way to care for your mule is to create as natural an environment as possible, coupled with what is realistic in today's society. Taking cues from horse owners, some new mule owners think like humans and not like mules when it comes to caring for their new friend.

These folks can believe that mules want what they want, which is their own space (a tiny box stall with minimal social contact), to be hand-fed regulated meals (two or three times a day feeding and watering), and to be without a job (minimal physical and/or mental exercise or stimulation). This way of thinking breeds terribly unhappy mules. And then these human-thinking owners wonder why they have ongoing mule problems. Mules are not humans, and it is dangerous to project your needs, wants, and desires onto your animal.

Caring for a mule is similar to caring for a horse. Let's talk horses for a moment. Jamie Jackson is a farrier who conducted a thorough examination of many wild horses in cooperation with the Bureau of Land Management over several years. He was able to study these horses in their natural habitat and came to some startling conclusions in regards to optimum care, health, and happiness for the domesticated horse. Jamie suggests some rather bold moves in creating that natural environment for your mule, his vision is enlightening and makes us think about equine care from another perspective. Below is an excerpt from his book, *The Natural Horse.*[20]

> *Tear down the stalls and fences and let the horses run about and mingle. Let them argue and fight—horses love to fight—but they like even more to work things out. Contour the pasture to get rid of all the flat spots. Then spread rocks of all sizes and shapes across the up-and-down pasture—and if the horse does not have to put its nose on the ground during the first day to see where it is going then keep tossing truckloads [of rock] around until it does. Next, abandon the use of the feed mangers and feed the horses on the ground...Pull the watering contraptions down off the wall and kick the water troughs over, and then water the horses at ground level so they will use their big, strong necks; make sure they have to stand in mud if they want to drink. Pull off the horseshoes—especially the ones with the "bars", and ride the horse barefooted until it is lean and muscular...*

> *...Lots of daily exercise is important and so is a variety of nutritious feeds. Because of its [the wild horse] freedom to move about, it is ensured a variety of foods to eat. Wild horses simply do not stand in one place at a feed box or hay manger to eat just one or two things. A good sized pasture containing a variety of plants and grasses known to be edible and nutritious to the horse is what we must strive to provide.*

Back to the mule now. In a perfect world, the smart human would consider presenting the mule with Jamie's suggestions. However, today, I don't think anyone is going to go out and contour their flat pasture to make it seriously uneven, bringing in tons of rock, even though it probably would be beneficial to the mule. Therefore, balance out what is best for them with what is reasonable for you to create for them.

When you begin chatting with others about mule care consistently and inappropriately, you will hear "mules don't need as much food or water as horses," "mules never get sick or lame," "mules won't ever colic," and "mules will stop eating when they're full, so ya don't have to worry about 'em." This leads a person to believe that mules do not require forethought in their care. *They do.* First, we will address the food and water that your mule deserves.

Food and Water

I strongly recommend treating your mule as you would a horse when it comes to the quantity and quality of feed he consumes. Feed as you would a horse of the same size and age. Remember, those young growing mules need more "groceries" than an adult mule. Make sure you provide him with a field that has a variety of nonpoisonous plants so he can forage to his heart's content!

My personal concerns on the subject of feeding are strong since I was one of the many who believed the misinformation (as stated above) which I heard or read in those horse books that had a tiny chapter regarding mules. Not knowing any better, I proceeded to underfeed my two-year-old molly.

At the time, all my animals were fed together in a big field. I intentionally doled out less hay to my molly mule, Sally, with the misinformed belief and understanding that being a mule, she didn't need as many groceries as her horse cousins did. At each feeding, Sally behaved typically of mules and ate her portion slowly. The two horses in the same field naturally consumed their hay quickly and then proceeded to chase Sally off and dine on her portion. It wasn't until I had the mule in another field and fed her separately that I realized she needed much more hay than I had been giving her. Besides, she was a growing two-year-old, which automatically requires more food.

 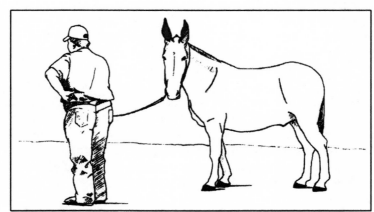

Illustration by Lori Mirmesdagh, Albuquerque, NM.

Quite often, the overweight mule has an overweight owner.

If I had been observant and educated at that time, I would have questioned why my molly was beginning to be too aggressive at the gate at feeding time. It was very difficult to keep her from grabbing mouthfuls of hay even before I entered the field. As I walked with her dinner towards the feeding area, Sally paced me exactly, and the grain bucket was constantly filled with a white mule nose no matter what I did to discourage her. Now, I will be the first one to recognize that a mule can be less discouraging than a horse when it comes to their dinner; however, there is tolerable and then there is intolerable!

When I began feeding my molly properly, her aggressiveness became less. Still, she would meet me at the gate, usually with a bray, to welcome my arrival. To both of our agreement, she was allowed to grab one bite of hay as I entered the field. I decided she could not have her nose inside the grain bucket, but she could follow with her nose one inch from the top of that bucket! That was to assure her that she had first grabs when I doled out the rations.

When her belly was full, I noticed that Sally would walk away from some of the less desirable stalks of hay. I have since learned to judge mule feeding amounts not by weight, not by volume, but by them telling me how much they need to eat. This can be done safely with grass hay, but not so accurately with alfalfa or other premium hay, since the mule may eat premium hay even when he is full. Please apply these observations with caution and common sense.

Watching his behavior can tell you the quantity of feed that is appropriate for your mule. Here is a rundown of underfed mule behaviors:

- Aggressive fighting amongst themselves when they see you coming to feed.

- Braying to excess. This also may happen if their mealtimes are inconsistent.

- Runs you over when you enter the field with the food. This may or may not be an underfed problem, depending upon the handler, the mule, and the training.

- All food is consumed at the first standing. Most mules will eat until full and then come back to eat more later. Remember, the equine's natural eating style is to graze on and off twenty-four hours a day.

- The backbone is prominently visible. The first sign of weight loss can be detected by a more noticeable backbone and a loss of fullness in the hindquarters. Soon after, there will be a showing of the ribs.

Here are some signs of overfed behaviors:

- No vocal greeting.

- Animals do not meet you at feeding time.

- Hay is left over from the last feeding.

- Young mules are too busy playing and don't get right to eating.

- Too big of a belly. No, that molly is not pregnant!

- Thick neck. Check the crest (top) of the neck to see if it is getting solid, thick, and inflexible, which can be the first sign of founder (a lameness caused by an extreme overweight condition).

On occasion, Sally would not eat her grain if there was something wrong with it. She was the one to tell me it was bad by refusing to eat a bit—a sign that maybe there was something in the grain that the human senses could not detect. The horses would eat the same bad grain nevertheless.

One footnote is that this feeding ritual is a bond between my critters and me. I may not always have enough time for them, but I usually keep myself in the position of caretaker. Sometimes in the winter, the main time I see my animals is at mealtime. When that is the case, I take along a rubber curry comb and brush them as they eat. I don't know what it does for them, but it sure makes me feel connected with them, the earth, and the whole life force—my assurance of sanity!

On water, it would be ideal if your pasture had a year-round fresh and clean flowing creek running through it. If it doesn't, please allow your mule as much clean, fresh water as he wants. Don't forget that the mule also needs free-choice natural salt and minerals, just like the horse or donkey. Salt blocks are designed for bovines with their rough tongues. Equines have smooth tongues, and your equine may not be getting his required dose of

Photo courtesy of Dianne Bailey, ShutterSteeds, Ashland, VA.
Photo of John, owned by Eddie Thomas, Milford, VA.

Even though a mule has free access shelter, it doesn't mean he will choose to use it when *we* think he should!

salt from a block or lick. If you find teeth marks in your salt block or lick, it may be an indication that the animal needs more nutrients than he can get from the block. If he is not obtaining the needed salt and/or minerals, his optimum health may be compromised.

Do your research on equine health companies, and make sure you offer your mule appropriate free-choice minerals from as natural of origins as possible.

Shelter

The very best housing situation for your mule is a free-access shelter. This is a shelter where your mule can go inside or not at his choosing. Have the shelter open to a spacious, grassy outdoors, with trees to boot, if possible. When mules have free-access shelters, they quite often will choose to use the shelter in the rain, snow, wind, or extreme heat, but like to hang out under the trees with their buddies on those milder days. Knowing that a mule in nature grazes and forages on and off throughout the day and night, a free-access shelter provides him with his choosing of when to graze and when to go inside. Freedom of choice is important to his health, happiness, and peace of mind.

Personally, I strongly disagree with box stalls for mules, just as I disagree with box stalls for horses. I agree that stalls are necessary in the case of keeping a temporarily sick or lame animal quiet for recovery purposes. I also agree that box stalls are appropriate for minimal-stay events when constant care is being managed and your mule is getting plenty of exercise, such as a show or other performance work away from home.

What I do not agree with is a box stall as a mule's primary home, one which the animal rarely sees other than from the inside out. If in doubt as to how you feel about such housing, put yourself in the equine's position. Would you like to see the inside of a ten-foot-by-ten-foot box for twenty-three to twenty-four hours a day with minimal room to move around? In the human world, don't we call these jail cells? How would you like to smell urine and feces as the usual aroma of the day? When his ancestry has been in the wild and totally free, how can any equine want a box stall as permanent housing? It is amazing to me what the equine has come to tolerate in his domesticity.

Did you know that out in the fresh air, an equine smells, hears, and senses many things that we humans cannot? In their ancestry, these smells, sounds, and feelings gave them vital information needed for survival. This provided peace of mind, joy, fear, curiosity, and other important emotions. These fine-tuned senses are still active today in our domesticated critters. Humans have a tendency to dismiss such sensitivity simply because we do not possess, or are not conscious of possessing, the same sensory input, and so have not realized how vital this information is to the equine for his peace of mind. It's simply part of a mule being a mule.

The structure of his free-access shelter need not be fancy, just enough to keep the snow or rain off and the heat of the day at a minimum. It also must have relatively dry footing and a windbreak. Interaction with other animals is important; however, the mule may have a tendency to become overly herd-bound (see Idiosyncrasies, Chapter 12).

When setting up shelter for your mule, there is one thing to keep in mind. If your mule will be housed with horses, more than likely the horses will be boss over the mule, and that means the horse(s) may chase the mule(s) out of a small barn. Please see that your mule has plenty of room inside to get away from a dominant horse without being trapped in a corner and possibly kicked or bitten. Consider building a second opening on the opposite side for a quick and easy mule escape when needed.

Grooming

Brushing is a way to gentle and build trust in an unsure mule. It feels so good to him, it is hard for him to resist. Brush your mule frequently, just as you do your horse. This doesn't mean a light passing over of the brush. For a proper grooming session, take a rubber (not steel) curry comb, and with plenty of muscle, move the comb in a circular motion all over his body. Once you have all the clumps of dirt off with the rubber curry, then go over with a stiff brush. Take your stiff brush and with quick, short strokes, brush from his ears to his rear and down his legs (make sure, prior to brushing his rear and legs, that you know your mule to be safe). The legs, especially below the knee or hock, are more sensitive, and a lighter grooming hand is in order in these sensitive areas. Next, repeat this quick-stroke procedure with a soft, bristled brush. This grooming procedure does more than bring out his natural body oils and make his coat shiny; you will be his massage therapist, and he will love it.

The mule's coarser mane and tail do not give to grabbing burrs and stickers as tightly as a horse's tail, and therefore it's easier to pull stickers out. Mules shed their winter coat out later in the spring than the horse, but not as late as the donkey. In some colder areas of the country, the donkey does not shed out at all. Do not be concerned if the coat on your mule seems to be expecting snow when his horse friend is prepared for the blazing sun. During the shedding phase, the mule's skin becomes itchy and he ends up scratching and rolling more than usual. Do your mule a favor. During these spring times, indulge his needs and give him a daily hair extraction with a shedding blade. He will appreciate it immensely, and tomorrow he will be in your back pocket in order to be the first one brushed!

In the mule's casual pleasure world (the show world may be different), it is appropriate for the mule to carry a roached (cut-off) mane and forelock along with the top three to six inches of the tail shaven. The end of the tail is usually cut horizontally around hock level. On mules that have flowing, horse-like tails, it is acceptable not to have them shaven on the top or cut off on the bottom. It is also okay to let the mule mane grow out, as long as it falls over and has the appearance of a horse mane. On many mules, the coarser mane will stand straight up no matter how long you let it grow. And do not try clipping a bridle path on a mane that does not fall over. It can look very strange!

Photo courtesy of Michelle Dirkse, Seattle, WA.

Here are a few supplies that are essential in caring for your mule properly.

Hoof Care

Mules can go barefoot in more instances than the horse. If you live in an area where the ground is fertile loam rather than rocky, and most all of your riding is in the arena or on soft footing, you may rarely need to shoe your mule. If you ride on any other surface for an extended period of time, it would be best to shoe him. With trail riding of more than a couple of hours, high-country packing, or pleasure driving on a surface other than paved roads, it would be wise to put shoes on for his protection.

Hoof cracks usually do not create lameness, as most are surface cracks. Do watch your mule closely if you notice he has cracks in his hoof to be certain he is not suffering in his travels. It is well known that white hooves are weaker and more prone to splitting, cracking, and chipping than black hooves. Most tack or feed stores have an abundance of products on the market to strengthen the hooves in horses. Mule hooves are naturally tougher than horse hooves. A good plan for inferior hooves is a bit of cooking oil mixed in with the daily grain ration of the mule. This not only works in strengthening the hoof from the inside out, but also helps bring out the shine in the coat of your mule.

110

There is another hoof problem to keep an eye out for, and that is a deterioration of the hoof wall, which can invite bacteria. This is known by many names, such as seedy toe, hoof rot, or white line disease. Prevention is the best cure by keeping hooves dry, clean, trimmed, and shod regularly.

The frog is the spongy material inside the hoof of your mule. If this frog becomes infected due to constant moisture from mud or manure in the hoof of your mule, it may lead to a degeneration of tissues, called thrush. You can readily smell thrush by a very rank odor when picking up his foot. The best cure, again, is prevention. Keep his feet clean, dry, and trimmed regularly. Using a treatment such as Koppertox®, a green liquid you can buy in most feed stores, can help the smelly situation. People have told me about using a mixture of equal parts of bleach and water or an iodine solution for the treatment of thrush, being careful not to get any of this solution on the mule's skin or the outside hoof wall. **NOTE**: Before you use any homemade treatment, please check with your veterinarian.

A mule, more than a horse, needs to have plenty of heel in his hoof. He will naturally be more upright in his stance than a horse, and keeping that heel is very important. Many farriers take way too much heel off mule hooves and need to be reminded to keep your mule in high heels. Some mule hooves grow slower than horse hooves, but they still need to be trimmed regularly. Do not forget to trim your donkey. We all have seen way too many donkeys and mules in fields with hooves so long that they begin to curl up on the toes. *This is totally unacceptable.*

Farriers

There are three essential ingredients in finding a good farrier or horseshoer: attitude, knowledge, and business sense.

ATTITUDE: A mule needs a farrier who exudes confidence, trust, and appreciation, rather than fear or cockiness. When interviewing to find a good farrier, ask him or her if she or he has ever worked with a mule and how she or he feels about mules in general. Some farriers are nervous and fearful working around a mule, which shines through loud and clear to the mule, who may be inclined to react unfavorably. Find a farrier who has previously trimmed up mules, if available. Ask around of their reputations. You don't want a farrier who handles mules abusively. (Firm, yes—abuse, no.) But also remember that your farrier is not a trainer. Please teach your mule to pick up, hold, twist, pull, and otherwise maneuver all four feet quietly, long before the farrier arrives.

KNOWLEDGE: Most farriers nowadays obtain their knowledge from accredited farrier schools, coupled with lots of experience. Don't be afraid of asking a prospective farrier for references. Take a look at the hooves of some horses (or mules, if available) that a prospective farrier has trimmed. If she or he has a habit of taking off the heel, be cautious in using him or her in trimming your mule. Also, a farrier may give you medical advice about your animal, as she or he probably has had schooling regarding the equine hoof. However, no farrier can take the place of a licensed veterinarian when difficult technical questions need to be answered.

BUSINESS SENSE: This service person should also know how to conduct business. I have found that in my area, farriers may not return phone calls, are consistently late, or simply fail to show up at all. How these less-than-perfect business owners keep their clients and stay in business astounds me, as the farrier competition around my geography is high. The most accurate advertising for any farrier is through word of mouth. Ask other local mule

Photo courtesy of Nancy Hawthorn, Flying H Farm, Sims, AR.
Photo of Grady Hawthorn and Margo.

Please make sure you have your mule trained to be calm and relaxed *before* the farrier arrives.

and horse owners, veterinarians, and feed stores for recommendations. Pay attention to what people say about their farrier on all three aspects. It truly is a prize to find one who knows how to conduct business properly, has a good attitude toward the equine and the mule owner, and is knowledgeable about how to trim and shoe. (Bonus points if he also knows corrective shoeing.) If you find a farrier who has all of the above three essentials, *keep him or her* and never let go!

If you know the farrier will show up on time, have your mule caught and his feet cleaned prior to the farrier arriving. Good farriers are in demand and usually very busy. It is frustrating to show up at a farm and then have to wait for the owner to catch that game-playing mule!

Miscellaneous Ailments

Equine veterinarians say that if their practice relied solely on mules, they would quickly go out of business! The following are thoughts and concerns in adequately caring for your mule. Living in the Northwest, I am most familiar with problems that rain and mud create. Please take this information as a general guide. Again, I am not a veterinarian, and luckily, I have not experienced many medical problems with mules. Always get advice from a qualified vet in dealing with any medical concerns.

- The mule doesn't seem to harbor as many diseases as the horse. Give your mules the same yearly shots and doctor them for injuries just as you would a horse (or as recommended by a qualified local veterinarian). It is possible to have an infection settle in the legs of the sickly mule. The mule *can* colic and founder. Remember to watch for any abnormalities in your mule and notify your vet if necessary. These ailments seem far less frequent than for a horse. Still, do not think your mule is invincible.

- A mule given anesthetic does not go under as deep as a horse and has side effects. *Absolutely use a veterinarian to judge the quantity of such drugs.* Usually you can treat a mule as a horse in regular preventative maintenance; however, I would question your vet as to his confidence in his ability to treat your mule properly.

- Occasionally, mules will get small and large hooks (sharp enamel points on the edges of his cheek teeth). A procedure known as floating the teeth can correct the small hooks. The large hooks need to be cut off with molar cutters. Have your vet check for hooks regularly. Be aware that a young, growing mule may have more teeth problems, as his teeth are growing and settling in. Signs that your mule is suffering from hooks:

- o   drops his grain irregularly
- o   has abnormal head shaking
- o   refuses a bit
- o   is losing weight unexpectedly

- Rain rot is scattered tufts of matted, crusted hair on the mule's back, withers, and rump. This is caused by an overabundance of rain or precipitation, coupled with lack of adequate shelter and lack of grooming. Rain rot can be prevented by allowing free-choice shelter for your mule and by drying and brushing him regularly. If he does get rain rot, you can wash the area with iodine shampoo or Betadine®. Disinfect the brushes that are used on a mule with rain rot so you don't spread it around to your other farm critters.

- Try hydrogen peroxide in cleaning out minor wounds. The bubbling action in peroxide will penetrate portions of the wound that water may

Photo courtesy of Timber Tuckness, www.prorodeoactive.com

No colic here. Mules love to roll—a lot!

not be able to reach. Nitrofurazone is a gel-type ointment that is great to use on minor wounds after you have cleaned them out. A can of Bag Balm is a necessity to have around for helping to keep flies away from wounds.

- Keeping flies away from your mule is difficult in the summer time. Fly masks will keep those irritating creatures off your mule's face. Now, if you decide to use fly masks, *please* realize what they are for and what they are not for. These masks are designed to be put on the mule in the morning only on those days that are prime for face flies. These masks are to be taken off when the flies begin to leave for the day, usually at dusk. Period. This is their purpose.

Too many people show their laziness by keeping these contraptions on their poor mules day and night for weeks or months on end. This is not their purpose and only shows owner ignorance and/or laziness in properly caring for the mule. Again, you have people thinking like people, not like mules. Have you ever had one of these on your face? Try it sometime and you will see what it does to your vision. It darkens and distorts everything you see. These masks make it difficult for your mule to adjust to the dark, such as when he enters a barn, and keeps him at a disadvantage with his sight at nighttime.

One short-term natural fly solution is to mix together:

- o 1 cup Avon Skin-So-Soft oil
- o 2 cups white vinegar
- o 1 Tbsp. eucalyptus oil
- o 3 cups water

You can use a rag to wipe this mixture on, or put it in a spray bottle and spray it on. Careful—a mule can be just as skittish as a horse when a spray is used on him. You must desensitize him so that ticklish mist is not something he feels he needs to run from. Just remember to mix or shake each time before you use it. I like to have a bucket of this nearby and wipe it on Sally whenever I go to see her. This works about as well as any on the market.

- Keep your pastures maintained properly—do not overgraze them. Hitch up that harness mule once a year and have him pull a harrow around your field to spread out the manure on a hot, sunny day. This does more than fertilize your land; it will also help prevent intestinal worms. I am not a technical person, as you can tell; however, to get the picture of the worm cycle, try this.

- Manure on the ground contains small, sometimes barely noticeable worms. They thrive readily in the moist manure, yet filter into the soil. Mules eat the grass growing in this soil and ingest the worms. Worms get into the mule's stomach and eat anything the mule has recently ingested. When that is gone, those ungrateful worms begin eating the walls of the stomach. They then travel out the rear by way of the manure and again filter into the soil to be ingested again. Harrowing on a really hot day will aid in breaking up this cycle and kill the worms living in the manure.

- Worming every six weeks is essential in mules as in horses. It is recommended to rotate your wormers. Wormers change and improve all the time, so ask your vet what is currently the best product and procedure for worming your mule in your area. A good idea is to set a worming schedule where you use the best available wormer as your main wormer every other time you worm and various other wormers as the rotators on the opposite worming times.

- Keep the little yellow bot eggs off your mule's legs and body. A bot fly is a bee-like creature that flies close around your mule and drives him crazy! The bot fly lays many yellow eggs which attach onto the hairs of your mule. A simple bot knife works pretty well to take them off and is less risky than using a pocket knife. Bot flies are fairly easy to hit with your open hand, knocking them to the ground to be able to step on them. Do use a wormer that takes care of bots *before* the bot season.

Special Three-Year-Old Attention

The three-year-old mule does need some special considerations that you may not have realized. Here again are wise words from the old-time master, Harry Riley, in *The Mule*,[7] concerning the three-year-old mule. What you read below is regarding heavily worked mules of that era.

A three-year-old mule may have many loose teeth in his mouth. At this age, a mule can be in worse general condition than he is at any other period in his life. At three, he is more subject to distemper, sore eyes, and inflammation of all parts of the head and body. Because of the changes he is undergoing, he is more apt to take contagious diseases than at any other time.

Do not buy three-year-old mules to put to work that requires a five- or six-year-old mule to perform. Six three-year-old mules are just about as fit to travel fifteen miles per day—with a loaded army wagon and their forage—as a boy six years of age is fit to do a man's work. The three-year-old mule would lie down and not eat a bite through sheer exhaustion.

A mule at three years old is just as much and even more of a colt than a horse is. And he is as much out of condition on account of his cutting teeth, distemper, and other colt ailments as it is possible to be. Get a three-year-old mule tired and fatigued and in nine cases out of ten, he will get so discouraged that it will be next to impossible to get him home or into camp. A horse colt will work his way home cheerfully, but the young mule will sulk. An honest horse will try to help himself and do all he can for you, especially if you treat him kindly. The mule colt will just as likely as not do all he can to make it inconvenient for you and him.

Older Mules

The average lifespan of a mule is thirty to thirty-five years. Average lifespan for a horse is twenty to twenty-five years, and with a donkey it is thirty-five to forty-five years. With good management, food, and medical care, owners can expect good solid work out of their mule up to the age of thirty or forty years old. In extreme old age, the mule is generally more useful than a horse of the same age.

Larry McKim, a veterinarian from Glendale, Arizona, recalls putting a forty-seven-year-old mule to sleep because it began to go downhill after it had been retired at age forty-five. "If they had kept on using it lightly, I'm sure it would probably have lived even longer," Dr. McKim said.

There you have it, the very best way to care for your mule.

CHAPTER 12:
MULE IDIOSYNCRASIES

"I GIVE UP, I'LL NEVER UNDERSTAND MULES!"

There is an old saying, "If a person thinks he knows everything about mules, he is sure to know very little about them." When it comes to noting strange mule behaviors, get out your endless scroll—as this list can become quite long. These unusual behaviors, known as idiosyncrasies, seem to defy human logic at times. To correctly interpret these idiosyncrasies, one must learn and understand the instinctual ways, natural habitat, and mindset of both the donkey and the horse, since the mule is a combination of both equines. When you research the donkey and horse heritage, you will learn a lot about why mules do what they do. This chapter will enlighten you about some mule idiosyncrasies.

The Natural Horse

Both the donkey and the horse have their particular ways and methods of survival, which have allowed them to live and prosper for thousands of years. We all are familiar with the environment and natural instincts of the horse, as there is an abundance of books, articles, and formal studies published on this subject. My research into the natural horse and natural donkey led me to Kelly Grissom, wild horse and burro specialist for the Arizona State Office of the Bureau of Land Management. Kelly gave me vital information on the wild equines of America in regards to natural habitat and behaviors. Here is a quick review of the horse.

Photo courtesy of Jason I. Ransom, U.S. Geological Survey, Fort Collins, CO.

Wild horses, "living symbols of the historic and pioneer spirit of the West", are legally protected by the U.S. government.

Horses have survived for years by roaming around on relatively flat prairie and grazing on the best grasses available. Horses travel many miles to find meadows to graze and do not have a particular territory—as does the burro. The home of the horse ranges many square miles. There is one stallion with his harem of mares and their offspring in a herd. The group travels together, with one of the mares as the boss. This boss mare keeps all horses in line with her strict discipline, and leads their travels. The stallion follows behind to make sure his herd stays together. Stallions fight with other stallions to keep or take over a herd of mares and foals—with the fittest stallion wining the prize. Kelly Grissom states:

> *Horses exhibit a social order known as the harem band—a single, dominant stallion and a closely guarded harem of females to whom he bonds and breeds. They travel together and the stallion protects his mares from any possible outside stallions, fighting them off if necessary.*

Horses are vegetarians and do not prey upon other animals. They fear being caught and killed by predatory animals such as the big cats, bears, wild dogs, and humans. In order for the species to survive, the horse must

119

behave in certain ways to ensure his safety. For horses, the foremost method of survival is by running away—or fleeing—from danger. When one horse in the herd hears or senses danger, she alerts the others and off they run with the boss mare in front.

The Natural Donkey

In trying to understand the mule, we also need in-depth information about the donkey and his natural life. This information was a bit more difficult to obtain. Kelly Grissom of the BLM pulled through and enlightened me about the natural donkey.

> *A donkey's natural environment is the desert. He fills his belly with brush, leaves, various plants, and grasses found in his natural desert surroundings and has learned to be a great forager. The donkey has not had the luxury of an abundance of water, so has adapted to live off of a minimal supply. Donkeys do travel in herds and are very loyal to each other. They take care of each other and will divide into smaller groups far enough away for minimal friction but never out of touch as a herd.*

The donkey, as the horse, does not prey on other animals. He fears being caught and killed by predatory animals, just like the horse does. The donkey has learned to quickly judge a dangerous situation and react accordingly, developing his fight instinct for those times of imminent danger. A donkey doesn't panic and flee like a horse; he will simply run far enough to take himself out of danger's way. In encountering predators, the donkey can tap into his developed defensive fight instinct by kicking, biting, or striking, or simply by outsmarting his enemy by hiding quietly in the brush of his coat color.

He also has his flight instinct available when necessary. In order to survive in his natural environment of rocky and hilly terrain of the low desert, one positive feature of the donkey is his small hooves and extremely good footing in case he needs to quickly escape a predator. If nature had not provided him with those tough, narrow hooves to ensure his surefootedness, a donkey, unstable in his footing, could become lunch for a predator.

Photo courtesy of Bureau of Land Management, Washington DC.

Wild burros still roam free in specific areas of the western United States.

Here is a summary of the donkey or burro from Kelly Grissom:

Burros are well adapted to a desert environment as they are descendents of the African Wild Ass. Their evolutionary tract led them to the very hot and severe desert climates of North Africa so the American deserts would be relatively lush compared to their standards.

Burros generally live in the southern United States where temperatures reach 120 degrees and have mild winters. Horses generally live in the northern climates where they are exposed to more severe winters.

The terrain where [today's wild] burros are found is mainly on the low deserts, usually at lower elevations than horses. Burros are found in areas of broad valleys and rough volcanic mountains. The terrain is tough to traverse for any species. Burros are very efficient in their travels. When working through the ridges, the burros' efficiency becomes apparent as they do not go straight up over a ridge but work up the slopes through a system of switch back trails that they have created. When walking in the desert, I usually walk along burro trails as I have found that they will find the easiest way to traverse the country.

Social order is a function of breeding efficiency, which leads directly to survival of a species. To maximize breeding efficiency in areas where forage is limited, groupings are small. The strongest group structure

121

in a burro's world is that of a jenny and her foal. You will see large groups of burros but the social bonding is minimal. They hang around with each other for company more than anything else. These groups may hang together for part of a day or for several days. Studs [jacks] will hang in groups but again, not a bachelor band like horses. These temporary bands will disperse and may reform with other participants as the forage permits. To increase the possibility of breeding an estrous female, a portion of the older males will set up territories along the trails usually leading to water. When an estrous female enters his territory, the stud [jack] then has exclusive breeding rights as she passes through. Outside of a territory, any male can breed her and intense fighting may occur. While burros may be fighting, other burros may stand in line to breed her.

Burros are docile by nature. Where wild horses and burros share the habitat, they have a tendency to live in like groups (i.e., horses with horses, burros with burros). But they do intermix in the wild with the reproduction of wild mules occurring. I have seen mules running with burros, exhibiting a harem behavior where they will be found with the same burro throughout the year. I have also seen mules running with horses in a harem environment.

I haven't seen any hinnies in the wild but they may occur. It may be because of the social structure where burros will breed any available estrous female they may come in contact with, while a horse will try to set up a harem. Since burros do not prefer harem behavior, it would be harder for a stud horse to control the behavior of a jenny long enough for him to breed her to produce a hinny.

How This Applies to the Mule

As stated, the donkey's metabolism is suited for the blazing desert sun, and he thrives readily in a hot, arid climate with minimal water. This explains why a mule can handle heat with absolute bearability—he is much more tolerant than his half-brother the horse. On the other hand, the horse is from a cooler climate and has a more thickened coat and hide, which is handed down to the mule. This provides the mule with endurance of the cold and wet climates. And for some reason, the mule handles this wet and cold climate much better than the horse.

Instincts: Flight vs. Fight

In the presence of immediate danger, the donkey has a tendency to fight first, run second, while the horse has a tendency to run first and fight second. The mule has both influences available to act upon. There seems to be no etched-in-stone rule for mules when posed with a threat. I have found some mules will fight in fear through kicking, biting, and sometimes striking. Yet, I have found mules who have a stronger tendency to flee at the very inkling of real or imagined fear. Be prepared to accommodate both responses in handling an unfamiliar mule.

A mule can forage much better than a horse thanks to the donkey side of his ancestry. Plus, he seems to derive personal joy out of it, especially when it frustrates his owner, such as when he munches on a beloved flower bed!

The horse may attempt most anything that is asked of him by his handler due to what is called "heart," the willingness to please, even if it risks his own safety and possibly his life. On the other hand, the donkey is self-preserving and will not put himself in any kind of danger, regardless of who has asked him! Often it seems the donkey decides not to do what is asked of him simply because he doesn't want to—period.

Illustration by Lori Mirmesdagh, Albuquerque, NM.

Yes, mules have "heart". If treated well, they are willing partners in most instances.

The combination of these two extremes, the horse willingness and the donkey unwillingness (at times), produces an animal that will do many things asked of him as long as it doesn't interfere with his own self-preserving instincts. The independent nature of the donkey and the mule creates keen judgment on what they can and cannot handle in the way of weight pulled, load carried, and hours worked. Remember, the mule is not a donkey, and he can exert himself too much, following the horse-heart side of him. Because he may not react like a horse, the uneducated human may assume his mule is dumb, stubborn, or mean. The truth is, mules are very smart. Here are some more informative facts about mule idiosyncrasies to help you to better understand our favorite critter.

Watch Your Small Livestock

It is a commonly known fact in the mule world that a mule and a donkey can possess a natural instinct to harm small creatures such as dogs, cats, goats, lambs, and even foals. Why the mule feels this strong instinct is not understood by humans. This urge manifests by the mule chasing, striking, and even picking up the smaller animal with his teeth and throwing it down on the ground with unquestionable force, even if merely through play or curiosity.

I learned firsthand of this instinct during a playday in which Sally and I participated. We all were having a great time playing several games, one of which was a goat-tying event. It was my turn to race Sally up to the goat, flip him on his back, tie his legs together, get back on Sally, and race to the finish line. All went well until I got off, squatted down, and began tying up the goat. Sally felt compelled—it seemed to be out of curiosity about this new small plaything—and attempted to strike or paw at the goat. This instinct was so powerful that she didn't even know that she had struck me on my back with that powerful front leg and knocked me over. She then continued to chase after the goat, who subsequently began running away from this "predator." Someone grabbed Sally in time before she reached the goat, yet our fun playday came to a screeching halt.

Years after that incident, and before his departure from our farm, Rubel, a Nubian goat, was one of Sally's favorite companions. One time, I had no other option but to put Sally and Rubel in a field of strange horses who desperately wanted to chase this small, unfamiliar, four-legged critter. Sally would provide a sanctuary for Rubel from these large predators by letting him hide under her belly, peering out between her front legs!

It is possible that a strike is just the mule's way of trying to touch the animal. We humans touch unfamiliar things to learn about them, too. Do watch your loose mule (or donkey) very carefully the first time you put him in with smaller critters, however. If possible, have a private area where such livestock can escape completely out of mule range, such as a corner of the barn where you can nail a strong board across high enough that the smaller livestock can travel underneath but low enough that the mule or donkey cannot cross or reach over to grab them. Usually around chest-height to the mule or donkey is adequate for this barrier.

Once these equines get used to the smaller animals and accept them, they usually can be trusted implicitly. The donkey and mule then can be excellent guards for sheep and goats since they will chase coyotes and other predatory dogs out of the field.

Domestic dog chasing seems to be a game with both the mule and the dog, as well as an instinct. Mules and donkeys love to chase dogs and rarely will allow a dog to chase their horse pasture mates into a frenzy, as some dogs enjoy doing. In fact, the dogs are the ones in jeopardy entering a field where there is a mule or donkey!

Illustration by Lori Mirmesdagh, Albuquerque, NM.

When housing a mule with smaller livestock, make sure there is ample room and opportunity for the smaller ones to escape out of mule's reach—just in case the mule gets bored.

You need to be aware of this instinct when you are leading a green, impulsive mule and a dog passes by. All of a sudden, you may find yourself jerked out of your boots by a mule chasing after this dog! When familiar, the mule can readily accept and enjoy the company of a dog.

Mule Ears

Take care when working around mule ears. If brought up properly, a mule loves to have his ears rubbed and stroked. On occasion, the inexperienced and/or abusive handler will "ear down" a mule. That means that in attempting to control the mule, the handler will painfully twist the ear to keep the head or body still. Or, the old-time method is to bite the ear with human teeth. The ear is extremely sensitive, and mules do not take kindly to this type of treatment. *This kind of treatment is totally unacceptable.*

I cringe whenever I hear of this happening, for there are other, much more effective and humane discipline methods. I can only view this behavior as abuse given by an uninformed, lazy, or angry handler. That one abusive incident may set the stage for the rest of the mule's life, in that no one may be able to peacefully handle the ears ever again. I have known mules that you could not get a bridle on because they refused to let any person touch their ears.

Flying Hooves

A mule is a natural-born kicker. This is the fight instinct of defense against enemies—real or imagined—coming from the donkey side. If trained and disciplined properly and not allowed this expression of aggressiveness, the mule can be just as safe as a horse to be behind. In Solving Mule Problems, Chapter 14, we will discuss a great technique for solving mule kicking problems.

Until you know the mule you are behind, just be aware that when afraid, angry, or asserting his authority or displeasure, a mule may kick. He has an uncanny ability to aim and rarely misses his target if he so desires. If a mule does not hit the intended receiver, then take it to heart that it was just a warning. I have seen a mule under anesthetics, with barely a recognition of the world around him, kick a bothersome dog—square—with the speed of lightning!

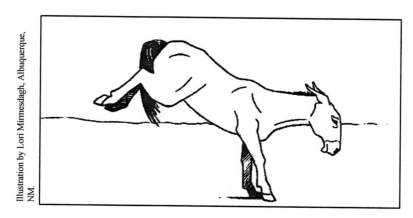

Illustration by Lori Mirmesdagh, Albuquerque, NM.

It's true, mules can kick. Quite often, they will intentionally miss the target, intending to only send a warning, or express dissatisfaction.

Also be aware that a mule and a donkey have the ability to cow-kick. A horse can kick forward or backward, but a mule can also kick straight out to the side. The best place to be around a kicking mule is on his back, and that still is no guarantee that you will not be touched!

SOME MULES KICK ALL THE TIME,

AND ALL MULES KICK SOME OF THE TIME!

It is said that a mule will kick a deserving person. He knows and understands intentional pain inflicted upon him. It is said that mules have the uncanny ability to accurately distinguish the fine line between discipline and abuse. The rumor has it that when abused, a mule may wait days, weeks, months, or years for just the right moment to nail the abuser. However, if the overall rapport with your mule is good, and you are just having an off day, he will generally forgive pretty quickly.

Gray Mares and Mules

What is all this talk about the attraction between gray mares and mules? Well, it seems that a mule becomes attached to gray or white mares more easily than you would imagine. When this attachment is solidly formed, it can be nearly impossible to separate them.

Ben Green, in his book *Horse Tradin'*,[21] tells a great story of various cowboys in the early 1900s buying this specific herd of wild mules from a horse trader. The purchasing cowboy would then round up his new mules and drive them off the trader's property, heading them towards their new home. The mules provided instant cash to the seller since he knew that these mules would automatically turn and come back to his land at a specific bend in the road just off his property. This allowed the shyster horse trader to keep the money for the mules and also keep the mules (using the reasoning, "It's not my fault you can't get these mules to your land").

Word got around to cowboy Ben Green about the antics of this shifty trader. Knowing the above fact about gray mares and mules, Ben was determined to catch the trader at his own game. He made arrangements with the sly seller to trade some heifers for the wild mules. Ben then arranged a gray mare to run with these mules for a few days until they formed this peculiar attachment. He then proceeded to drive the gray mare off the land, past the turn-around bend, and on to his own farm, with the not-so-wild mules following the gray mare like children!

Mule Dependency

The dependency of the mule is an important concern. If you have the best mule ever, but you cannot take him away from his buddy, you have a mule that sometimes borders on useless. Mules can become so attached to a horse, another mule, or any other animal, that they will go through, over, or under any fence to get to this buddy when separated. This is especially true in the case of young mules. If taught to be separated when young, this problem does not become any more of a hassle than with a horse. When separated from his buddy, an independent mule may run the fence line a bit but will quickly settle down.

If you have an older mule that is dependent upon a buddy, realize that he may never overcome his fear of being alone. If needing to separate the two, you can sometimes transfer the dependency onto other animals. A substitute such as another mule, horse, cow, donkey, familiar goat, or dog may do the trick. On a positive note, mules that run together as buddies will usually work well in a team.

Instinct, Intelligence, or Game-Playing?

It is important to recognize the subtle differences between instincts, intelligence, and game-playing to better judge the actions of your mule and respond accordingly.

INSTINCTS are impulsive actions that are not consciously decided upon by the mule. These acts are impulsive, focused, and require an abundance of time, patience, and firmness by the handler to overcome them. Some natural instincts to be aware of in dealing with the mule are:

- A garden hose, rope, or anything moving on the ground near him may simulate a dangerous snake and scare him.

- Things dragging or pulling behind him may simulate a predator that is after him, and frighten him. (The main reason for using blinders in driving is so the mule can't see what's behind him.)

- Something slightly above him may simulate a predator ready to pounce. An extension of this is to always teach your young mule that it is okay for you to be above him—such as sitting on a fence next to him—before you mount up for the first time.

- Taking him away from his buddies is threatening, as he believes that there is safety in numbers. For example, let's say you are leading a mule and he balks when you take him away from his buddies. This forced separation is a human decision, and the mule's herding instinct tells him to stay with his friends. This mule will probably stop and refuse to move one more inch away from his buddies. He is simply reacting out of instinct. It is not wrong, nor is he being stubborn. He merely is protecting himself the way nature has taught him.

Caution is in order in getting him over instincts. After you have figured out with your training methods what it takes to overcome obstacles with your particular mule, use the method quickly and determinedly the next few times when instinct is his obstacle to insure that game-playing does not start. The mule may be testing you to see if you are serious about your decision. If you are unsure, the mule will certainly say "no." In short, the mule will mirror your own confidence.

On the **INTELLIGENCE** side, realize that the mule may very well be thinking faster than you. Be sure that what you think is game-playing is not your smart mule's way of telling you that something is wrong. If he thinks he is not being heard, the mule may try to communicate more forcefully. The intelligent handler first tries to figure out why the mule seems to be misbehaving.

For example, one mule in for training always balked just as I led him onto our driveway. This new, unfinished drive was full of sharp base rock and lacking the top layer of fine gravel. This driveway hurt his bare feet. An unassuming owner would never connect the rocks in the driveway with possible pain and would just chalk it up to "mule stubbornness." In getting him to walk on the rocks, I would verbally tell him, "I know the rocks hurt and I'm sorry, but we have no other choice but to walk on them" (yes, they hear and understand you), and then I would follow with a gentle but firmly decisive move-forward technique that I had previously taught him. Confidence is the key, and once you are sure about yourself, rarely should you have serious battles with this method.

One other incident was when Sally wouldn't load into our two-horse trailer. She usually is a great trailer loader; however, it was obvious to me that her spontaneous resistance of cooperation was not game-playing or fear, but something actually seemed to be wrong. It wasn't until I emulated her actions by walking up into the trailer myself and sticking my nose in the manger, as I was asking her to do, that I realized there was smelly, moldy hay in the rusty, wet corner of the manger. After a thorough cleaning, she then gladly loaded into the trailer.

GAME-PLAYING is harder to identify. Most folks assume the behavior is game-playing when actually there may be a very good reason your mule is acting up. When you really know your mule and have a pretty good relationship with him, then it's easy to identify his bag of game-playing tricks. When working an unfamiliar mule, the best you can do is be prepared with your mule logic, give him the benefit of the doubt at first, and then, if you still cannot find a logical or fear-based reason for his actions, it should be safe to insist on him behaving in your way.

Telepathic Communication

We may find there is more to these wonderful creatures than our intelligent human mind can figure out. Here are a couple of stories that do not belong in any of the above categories.

For the first few years I owned Sally, I would load her into my two-horse trailer on the right-hand side. There was no particular reason for this, just habit through trailer loading problem horses, I suppose. Her trailer-loading behavior became increasingly resistant and difficult. One day, it became next to impossible to load her up. Her behavior wasn't game-playing, it wasn't instinct, and nothing seemed to really be wrong. I was baffled why she resisted. With one frustrating incident after another in trying to load her up, I finally called an animal communication specialist—a psychic. Lydia Hiby (see Suggested Readings) and others have the fabulous ability to get into animals' minds and tell us what they are thinking. Lydia told me that Sally wanted to be loaded on the left. That's just the way she was. And if she ever worked as a team, she also wanted to be on the left-hand side. Sally then loaded beautifully on the left side of the trailer, with no further resistance to this day.

My older Appaloosa horse, Zip, wasn't eating very well. This was unusual

Photo courtesy of Mary Bloodsworth, 3JM, Bonham, TX.

The bond between mule and person is evident in this photo of
Johnny Bloodsworth and Fran.

for him, as food was his best friend. It was wintertime and all the horses and mules were in a field that had free-choice shelter. We fed morning and night, but Zip never ate well on the night feeding. Another call to Lydia informed me that my aging Zip had night blindness, and he wouldn't go into the barn to eat after dark since the "doorway" was low and he had hit his head one too many times. We rigged up a light at the doorway, and Zip began eating his full night feeding again.

Emma was probably the most dramatic case that Lydia helped me with. Emma was a pack mule out of a thoroughbred mare who was brought in for a tune-up, as the owner called it. This sixteen-hand mule did not like having a pack saddle put on her back. Emma seemed to have absolutely no trust or interest in humans. The first thing I noticed was that Emma needed to have her long front feet trimmed up. I brought a farrier out to trim up her toes, but no luck. She would bolt, kick, and do anything she could think of to get that horseshoer away from her. I then arranged to have the vet out at the same time as the farrier for a second try. The vet sedated her three times (*ABSOLUTELY DO NOT TRY THIS AT HOME, as this quantity could kill an equine*) to even get her calm enough to pick up her front feet for a quick trim.

I worked with Emma for six months. Seemed I would get a pack on her back, have great hopes for her training, and she would then spontaneously freak and bolt away. After reaching the end of my rope, I decided to call Lydia as a last option, knowing that if I gave up training Emma, she would probably end up with a canner and used as dog meat. Lydia told me that Emma was in pain. Her whole back was out of alignment, and the most troubled area was near the base of her tail.

That explained why she would seem to be okay until I touched her on her withers or back and then she would bolt away. This also explained why she had long front feet. She literally could not hold up her front feet without her back feeling intense pain. And the complete lack of trust in humans developed because humans would hurt her every time they touched her.

I quickly took Emma to a vet who specialized in alternative medicine. "Dr. Bob" Anderson of Polk Veterinarian Clinic in Dallas, Oregon, confirmed that her problem was above the tail and put magnets on her to realign the spine. Magnets were used as an alternative to acupuncture needles—which certainly would have pained her even more—to obtain a rebalancing of her energy system. This helped her to balance out emotionally as well as physically. Within a week, Emma was out of pain. I could touch her body all over without her bolting or even cringing. I worked six more months on building trust on this seven-year-old crazy pack mule, and found out how difficult it is to retrain the memory of the older mule when pain is involved. After two additional years of daily mountain packing, I was pleased to hear that Emma turned out to be one of the outfitter's best pack mules on the string.

CHAPTER 13:
TRAINING MULES

"HOW DID YOU GET HIM TO DO THAT?"

Hmm…how do I explain the philosophy of proper mule training? Training is primarily accomplished through experience and instinct (i.e., mule sense). I try one thing, and if that doesn't work, I try another. Since there was so little information on mules at the time I was learning, you might say I attended the "School of Hard Knocks" at Mule University. I hope to fill you full of mule information so you will have an easier time in working with your mule. Nowadays, there are many more resources available on the psychology, philosophy, and training of mules through books, videos, and an abundance of mule experts. Nevertheless, my one-sentence advice for the prospective mule handler/trainer is, treat him as a horse and be prepared for anything!

As a reminder, for clarification, "handler" means anyone who handles the mule, be it owner, rider, driver, hired hand, or professional trainer. "He" is used for both male and female mules and their handlers just to simplify the information given.

Mule Wisdom

Webster defines wisdom as "the best means for attaining the best ends." Wisdom is what you obtain through experience, research, and practice. It is knowing the right things to do so the mule tries and is willing to please.

Photo courtesy of Katrina Walker, Wilson Creek Plowing Days, Wilson Creek, WA.

In training a young mule to drive, it is beneficial to sandwich the youngster between two broke mules.

How-to techniques quite often give one solution to one problem. When you have acquired wisdom, you can offer many solutions to many problems. Hopefully, I am providing you with a bit of mule wisdom so you have a good base to fall back on when how-to techniques fail.

Here are a few suggestions. Let that smart mule train himself whenever possible. Teach him to move away from your pressure—which is opposite of his natural inclination. Understand how he thinks, why he does what he does, and work with that information until you can get him to willingly give you what you want. Value and respect him, as he deserves the benefit of the doubt—unless he proves to you he doesn't. Listen to him for his suggestions and then make an educated decision. If you are asking for reasonable action, insist until you get it.

Profile of a Good Trainer

If you own a young mule, at some point you need to decide whether to train him yourself or send him out to a professional trainer. You may or may not be the perfect candidate to train your mule. Like it or not, if you handle a mule, you are a trainer who is teaching that mule something, either good or bad, all the time. If you have handled your youngster for the last year or two, you have learned about him and he has learned about you. You have asked him to do things and he has responded. You have worked with him and educated him since you two have been together. Today, look at your mule. How have you done? How is his attitude? Is he willing or not? Where do you have problems with him? How are his skills developing? This will tell you if you are on the right path to continue further with in-depth and more hazardous training, or, it may lead to a realization that your ways are not quite working in the way you would like and outside professional assistance with training your mule would be preferable. Also, if you are having challenges with your mule, you most likely are part of the problem, and educating you so you can better work together with your long-eared partner may be the best way to go.

A good mule trainer—you, or a professional—needs to have certain qualities for successful results. One of these qualities is a strong will. The handler needs to know what he wants clearly. He needs to be and stay in control of the situation (be the leader). He needs to be able to ask for what he wants, expect certain results, and praise when he gets them. The trainer is responsible for teaching your mule the difference between right and wrong and for setting up the situation so the mule will cooperate willingly when asked. And the trainer is also responsible as to how that mule views people—as pushovers, mean, or scary, or as respected and loved.

Horses are likely to become somewhat predictable in behavior when handled. However, this is not necessarily so with mules. No one really knows all the reaction possibilities of mules. If you find conflicting information, it may be because different mules can react in different ways to similar situations.

In choosing an outside person to train your mule, please be careful— not all horse trainers are mule trainers. One rule of thumb to judge a prospective mule trainer is to listen to him talk. If he has an arrogant, know-it-all attitude about mules, you can be sure he is far from knowing much about the mule. Such people have limited beliefs on how they think things should be and usually are closed off to new ideas. In this day and age, new ideas, opinions, and information are abundant. Some ideas or opinions aren't worth much, but every once in a while, there will be priceless gems which make training easier and better for mule and trainer both.

136

Illustration by Lori Mirmesdagh, Albuquerque, NM.

You can help your mule to accept weight and bulk on his back by
hanging same size and weight of tires on each side.

Choose a professional equine trainer who loves mules (even if he has never
trained a mule before), as he will be more apt to treat

them with respect and firmness. This trainer will probably give your mule
the benefit of the doubt. Find a trainer whose focus is on producing a
quality mule rather than on how much money he will make. Reputation is
everything in the training business, so don't be afraid to seek out mules and
horses that he has trained previously. You will learn a bundle about the
trainer's ability if you talk to the owners of his schooled equines.

Lots of people can train a horse, but it takes a true professional to train a
mule properly, as they are very intelligent. Most mules have quietly figured
out the trainer before he even enters the ring! And if the trainer isn't quick
with his thoughts and perceptions, the mule will have him running around in
circles in no time, with a big smile on that mule's face!

All trainers have their personal training style that works best for them. The
ideal style is where the journey to the desired end is painless and
encouraging, and the mule's development is willing and progressive.
Besides, the mule appreciates it when he connects with a human who listens

to him, understands how he thinks, and challenges him to grow. Look for a trainer who will enjoy taking on the challenge of training a very smart animal.

As you know, some handlers have a tendency to use force, pain, and/or fear tactics to get results. Resorting to force, fear, or pain usually is the product of the handler's repressed anger and fear. Using these methods makes him feel big and powerful, hurting that which he considers "lower than humans" in efforts to unload his inner anger and fears. To me, our critters are the most godlike of all of us, as they are the ones who have unconditional love down pat, along with immediate forgiveness and true friendship. Why not learn from them and try to live up to their standards of unconditional love instead of misusing their gentle, loving nature as a dumping ground for human emotions?

Sometimes a handler using these cruel methods is simply lazy or uneducated. Force and pain don't accomplish much with the mule and usually create resentment and resistance. Mules do not appreciate it and will not perform as well in the long run with this type of training, since force, fear, and pain usually become a training style rather than a one-time occurrence. We may not be able to help the angry or lazy handler. We now can help the uneducated handler, but only if he wants to further his understanding of the mule for peaceful and willing results.

Love, Discipline, and Timing

One essential feat to accomplish in working with your mule is to gain his friendship and respect. As in all animal training, genuine love and affection coupled with appropriate discipline will take you a long way. Handlers showing these qualities more than likely will produce a great mule with heart. And if ownership is transferred, the mule should initially view the new owner with the same respect. That new owner and his mule will soon develop their personal relationship, the quality of which is primarily dependent upon the new owner's attitude.

Sometimes you will find a one-person mule, working ever so willingly for that one person yet fighting the next. If you have acquired a mule that works well for his previous owner but you can't get him to do the same things in a peaceful manner, maybe you have not yet earned his respect and friendship. These long-eared creatures are social animals and appreciate your love, attention, and firmness.

A MULE UNDERSTANDS THE WORD NO.
HE TELLS HIS HANDLER THAT MANY TIMES!!

Discipline is a very important aspect of training your mule. Certainly don't be afraid of telling your mule "NO." Being too easy is just as detrimental to your mule as being too harsh. The perfect balance between too easy and too harsh comes only when you know your own personal boundaries or limits. This means you are very clear about what you will and won't accept from your mule and can communicate this simply and effectively to your four-legged partner. All mules will push to find your boundaries (the place where you will say "no"), so they know how far you will let them go. It's natural and it's okay. Horses, dogs, other pets, and people do it, too. For the most part, your mule doesn't care where your boundaries are, just as long as you have them and enforce them.

When your boundaries are crystal clear in your head, then your mule is much less apt to challenge them. No is a very clear and desirable word to your mule when spoken with conviction. Some people have a tough time saying "no" and feel that any equine, pet, or human is bad for putting them in a position where they need to say that dreaded two-letter word. They would rather think that their mule is trying to manipulate them or is being a bad mule and trying to create undue problems. Not so; these mules are simply learning what they can get away with and what they can't. Of course, if you are not clear and consistent about your boundaries or limits, then your mule surely won't know them either. A mule understands a solid, decisive "no" much better than he understands "Oh, come on now, quit it" or "Please don't do that...I'll get ma-a-a-d." This may work with a horse, but a mule is laughing at you inside, saying, "I got you, sucker!" when he hears these wishy-washy words.

When a mule pushes over your personal boundaries, all you have to do is put him back in line quickly and effectively, and then forget it. It's actually pretty simple. Besides, this practice just may allow you the confidence to say "no" in other areas of your life—if that seems to be an issue with you!

Photo courtesy of Michelle Dirkse, Seattle, WA.

Loading the mule seems to be an easier task if the trailer has a large opening with lots of room inside.

For example, let's say you find a mule that is determined to walk real close to you and nearly on your feet while you are leading him. Whose fault is it that he is walking on you? Is this his fault for behaving in this manner or yours for allowing him to behave in this manner?

A MULE WILL QUESTION YOU UNTIL YOU ARE SURE OF YOURSELF

As with humans, a lot of behaviors are from instincts or upbringing. Usually a young mule will walk close to you out of insecurity—as a foal does with his mother for protection. It is time he outgrows this behavior. Teach him not to walk on top of you by *simply not allowing it* in whatever clear, direct, and effective method you choose. You can also help him to find the security he needs and wean him off this mothering dependence by walking with one hand touching—not pushing—the crest of his neck.

One vital message on patience: keep your cool at all times. If you want to win the battle with your mule, the only effective way is by using your brain, not your brawn. Whenever you cannot get what you want out of your mule, it may be because you have not communicated your thoughts clearly enough. The moment you lose your patience, he has won the battle *and* knows how to win all subsequent battles to come. If you are at the point of losing it, gather up as much of your self-restraint as possible and walk away. Don't put the mule back in the field, as the mule will win then, too. Tie him at the source of the problem, walk away, cool down, think of a solution where you can get what you want or simply change your wants to a lesser outcome, then go back after a few minutes (never for any longer than this) and get that lesser outcome. And then go on from there. It's a kind of standoff, where you win a little and build on today's results tomorrow.

For example, say you want your mule to load into a trailer and he has a fit and decides he is not going to load. After an hour of trying to load him, you realize he is playing games with you and your patience wears thin. Before your temper blows and you start to whip him into the trailer (by the way, this is *never* the way to trailer load a mule), tie him right there at the trailer and walk away for a minute. This will enable you to cool down, think of a solution, and allow him time to think about what is happening. You may need to let down your ruffled ego and decide that you may not get him fully into the trailer today. Maybe you need to change today's goals from getting him into the trailer to having that wild and crazy mule stand quietly with all four feet outside of the trailer, with just his head inside it. You still have won for today since you have progressed from mass defiance to relaxed willingness to stand with his head in the trailer. Tomorrow, you can change that goal to having him put one foot in the trailer. The next day you may get two feet inside, and the next day all four.

Timing is another vitally important factor in training a mule. What that means is that your response to his behavior has to be immediate and firm. If you have a mule that does the unthinkable, that is, kick or bite at you, then you have my permission to be downright mean and nasty to him for *three seconds* after the event. After three seconds, he forgets why you are punishing him. Besides, it only takes that span of time to get the message across that his behavior is totally unacceptable around humans. In other words, reacting immediately creates the best impact and the most complete understanding.

Illustration by Lori Mirmesdagh, Albuquerque, NM.

A well-trained mule is essential when it's the
human who needs the training!

Training the Human

Many handlers don't expect to learn much from a mule, so therefore, they
don't. However, if you believe these smart equines can be your personal
tutors, they rarely will let you down. You must have a touch of humbleness
to accept mule teachings. Remember that the mule knows more than the
human in these instances:

- how to keep himself from getting hurt

- how to survive in the wild

- how his particular mind works

- how to get what he wants from his handler

- how much work is just right for him

The Psychic Mule

Ever wondered why your critters act one way today and another way tomorrow? Have you seen "moods" in your animals? Quite often your pets, equines, and farm animals are showing you how *you* are feeling by reacting to your emotions. Mules, as with most animals who are close to humans, are psychic and readily feel your emotions. The mule picks up strong emotions the easiest, such as when you are upset, sad, fearful, frustrated, confident, trusting, peaceful, and loving. Because this "picking up of emotions" is natural, it is difficult for him to understand when he can't get through to you. The mule works extremely hard in trying to be heard. If one way doesn't seem to get through, the mule will try another. You must be open-minded enough to listen to your teacher.

Just as we humans expect the mule to cooperate and work with us, the mule expects the handler to cooperate and work with him. It is our responsibility to be sensitive and knowledgeable enough to:

- Accept the mule as nearly an equal (there are rarely any 50/50 partnerships in the mule-human world. The human must be the leader with the mule a close second, say, 60/40).

- Work hard on trying to figure out what he is saying to you.

- Weigh the mule's messages and ideas against your own judgment to learn to work together.

Also along these lines, mules will work off the pictures in your mind more so than the words you say. If you say, "You will go through that gate," but you are picturing the mule balking, the mule will probably balk at the gate. To get the most effective response out of your mule, be aware of the pictures in your mind. When you see the mule balking at the gate in your mind, change that picture to seeing the mule walk through the gate easily. Now, this is not as easy as it sounds. This exercise will make you more aware of your true feelings (i.e., that you really expected the mule to balk at the gate) and give you some insight as to why you may not be getting what you want out of your mule. (Or, in truth, the mule is doing exactly what you expect, but not necessarily what you want.)

Again, when you want something from your mule, form the positive mental picture and wording. The positive picture is the picture of what you want

143

from him, not the picture of what you don't want. Follow the same procedure with the positive wording. Instead of saying, "Don't paw the ground," say, "Please stand quietly." Picture that quiet standing pose in your mind. It may not get him to stand quietly; however, it is much more likely that he will understand what you want from him. It is then up to him to decide if he wants to stand quietly or not. Now, if you picture him pawing in your mind and tell him not to paw, in effect, that is telling him it is okay to paw.

Also, take a look at the children you reared. If they are well disciplined, respectful, loving, and caring, more than likely you will raise a mule with the same attitude. If your children are unruly, troublemakers, or spoiled brats, you may find yourself with the same type of mule.

Imprinting

If you raise mules and are serious about solving those troublesome mule problems, you will learn the fine art of imprinting. Early foal imprint training is a process of handling your mule in every which way and in all places as a newborn foal. Proper imprinting will ease the natural fear of the mule, adding more willingness and creating a better attitude. Therefore, imprinting sets the stage for an adult mule to not have nearly as many typical mule problems, such as picking up feet, kicking, ear shyness, leading, tying, and being restrained. Imprint training is done as soon as possible after the birth of a mule foal, preferably prior to his first stand. *Imprint Training of the Newborn Foal* by Dr. Robert M. Miller (see Suggested Readings) is a great how-to book on these procedures.

Learning From the Older Mule

Listening to your broke and willing mule is especially important. If he decides he will not travel in a certain area, chances are he is trying to tell you that something is wrong. He probably knows more than you with his sensitive sixth sense. If you do not listen, he will try to get through to you stronger and louder. This may do one of two things: either an argument will ensue and one of you will give in to the other in a win/lose outcome; or you will acknowledge that he is trying to tell you something, reevaluate the situation and your original decision, and then act smartly on this new information. Given respect, a good mule will be very willing to work for you today and in the future.

One fact the handler will realize in dealing with older problem mules is that once a problem has escalated to create much turmoil, it can be very difficult to overcome these bad habits. A professional mule trainer may be able to get the mule to work well for him; however, usually far more time is involved in correcting established problems than is financially beneficial for the owner. And this still does not guarantee the owner will get the same results obtained by the trainer. A better plan would be to find a very knowledgeable mule trainer who is willing to teach you and the mule together. Just know that much of the teaching may need to be with *you*!

CHAPTER *14:*
SOLVING MULE PROBLEMS

The whole of this book is to help further you along in obtaining mule wisdom to be an informed problem solver when it comes to challenges with your mule. I had previously decided to not write specific how-to instructions in training your mule. Nevertheless, my desire has been overshadowed by reader demand for step-by-step instructions on certain tasks. Therefore, I have surrendered to write as best I can about a few techniques that have worked to solve some of the most common mule problems.

Every once in a while, a smart mule may learn a few more things than intended and need a bit of retraining. Here are a few special considerations that mules have which horses don't necessarily seem to share, at least not to the same extent.

Fix a Problem? Well, How Old Is He?

Age is a factor in retraining mules. A hurtful or scary incident with a young mule can create problems—sometimes for life—because of the mule's grand memory. Most mule problems can be corrected if the mule is young. If the mule is older and the problem is young, you still have a good chance of easily correcting this new habit of his. Only when the mule is older and the problem has been with him for quite some time is it overly difficult and/or hugely time-consuming to retrain him. Every once in a while, you find a

146

mule who has a problem so ingrained it is nearly impossible to change his behavior. These set-in problems may possibly be worked around.

For instance, one older mule worked his heart out during pulling contests. He and his buddy competed successfully in pulling massive weight atop a sled. This mule's problem was that no one could touch his ears to put a bridle on him. So, after many fights and many losses, the smart owner finally gave up and allowed him to pull with only a halter on his head, as you don't need to feed the ears through a halter as you do with a bridle. This worked for both the mule and the owner. The only difference was that this mule had to be trained to pull without blinders, which certainly didn't hinder his performance and seemed to be fine with both mule and owner.

Before You Mount Up

On solving problems, the mule needs to accept three things before he is a great mount.

1. He needs to accept that a human on the ground is higher up on the pecking order than he (most aggression toward humans, such as attitude, kicking, and biting problems, stems from this).

2. He needs to accept all tack as part of his being, with no fear of any of it (also see "Forbidden Fruit," later in this chapter).

3. He needs to accept a rider as non-threatening and perfectly fine to be on his back. This means you can jump on him bareback with no bridle in an open field and feel safe.

Many problems arise from these three things if they are not taken care of properly in the groundwork stage of his training. When you have the groundwork in order, there are three basic reasons a mule doesn't cooperate.

1. He doesn't know what you want.

2. He knows what you want but doesn't want to do it (some call this "stubborn").

3. He is afraid.

Most people jump to the "stubborn" conclusion when their mule is not cooperating. More often than expected, he doesn't know what you are asking or is afraid. Whenever you are trying to accomplish a goal with an

147

uncooperative mule, you must devise an intelligent scheme where he chooses to be a willing participant. The following set-up, wait, and reward system is an excellent method when the mule is not cooperating due to his strong free will, and also works well with a mule that doesn't know what you want.

Set Up, Wait, and Reward

The key to training success is:

- knowing why your mule is resisting,

- respecting him for his decision,

- deciding the most appropriate solution, and

- setting up it up so he will resolve his own problem in your desired manner.

The techniques that work for me all derive from a frame of mind, a philosophy, which I would like to share with you. This essential frame of mind is that you are going to let the mule train himself. You first must

Photo courtesy of Mark Schrimpf, Bar S Performance, Krum, TX. Mark on Chaparita.

Set up, wait, and reward is a slick method to allow the mule to make up his own mind, and to decide to respond in *your* desired way.

understand that a mule learns quickly and willingly if given the proper situation, and retains knowledge much better if he trains himself.

This form of wisdom is what's called "set up, wait, and reward." This is to create the desire in your mule to choose to do what you want him to do, that is, to stop what he is currently doing, change course, and choose to do it your way—which is the easiest way for him. In order for your mule to decide to behave in your desired way, he has to follow these steps:

- Encounter a situation where he questions his current decision and behavior.

- Explore other options.

- Decide upon the path of least resistance (which happens to be what you want from him).

- Do it.

It is a very simple idea but not easy to accomplish. Just as humans do, mules will naturally choose the path of least resistance (also known as laziness). You need to set it up so the path of least resistance is your chosen path. In your mule's deciding phase of this set-up, make sure you allow him time to explore any other options and to choose for himself which option he prefers. That is where your patience comes in. Now, if the situation is set up correctly, it will take minimal time for him to decide on your desired option. One message on this: you must know exactly what you want from your mule. Look at the overall picture, break it down into step-by-step goals, and ask your long-eared friend to accomplish these goals one step at a time. This generally works better than asking for the overall picture the first time around.

Go Left, Mule, Go Left!

Let's explore this "set up, wait, and reward" with an example. Let's say you are riding your mule and you want him to go left, yet he wants to continue to travel straight ahead. You are trying to neck rein him to the left and he stiffens up his neck and continues to go straight. Before you get frustrated and yank on his mouth with the reins, think of how you could get him to *decide* to go left.

First, why does he want to go straight? Is there something towards the left that he is afraid of? Or is going to the left going to get him into a dangerous situation? Or is it simply that straight is the direction of the barn and he wants to go home? Okay, you have determined there is no danger that he is trying to tell you about in going to the left, and straight ahead is the much-desired barn. Now you need to set up the situation so he will go left—willingly. We know the mule will naturally follow where his head is pointed. This is the path of least resistance. If you can get the head pointing to the left, then the body will follow eventually.

This method will work as long as you have a simple snaffle (or a straight-bar) bit in his mouth—*no shank and/or curb chain* for this example. If you don't happen to have a snaffle or straight-bar bit in his mouth, stop and change bits immediately. Or, just forgo the lesson for now and take time after your ride is over to change bits and find a place where you know he will resist your chosen direction, and then work through this problem.

At that moment of the battle of wills, loosen your grip on the right (oft) rein. With the proper bit in his mouth, take a tight hold of the left (near) rein and pull so the mule's head is bent strongly to the left. Put the near rein solid on your left knee and hold it (the *set-up*). Don't yank, yell, threaten, or attempt to stop your mule. Let your rein, hand, and leg just be solid (see illustration). Allow your mule to pull all he wants against the rein that is solid in your hand riding on your knee. Soon, he will question his current decision to go straight, as that isn't working for him with his head turned to the left (accomplishing step 1 above.)

GIVE A MAN A FISH AND YOU FEED HIM FOR A DAY; TEACH A MAN TO FISH AND YOU FEED HIM FOR A LIFETIME.

It is okay even if he decides to travel straight with his head rubbernecked to the left. He is exploring other and all options available to him—step 2 above. Just keep the rein solid on your near leg and *wait, wait, wait* until he gives in to the pressure and decides on the path of least resistance—to go where his head is pointed—step 3 above. Soon he will take that first step to straighten himself out, which will include one or more steps to the left—step 4 above. Immediately, with pinpoint timing being essential, at the exact moment of the first positive step, let go of the rein in your left hand to *reward* him for choosing that direction and praise him for his choice.

Again, your responsibility is to **set up** the situation, **wait** to allow the mule time to decide what to do, watch him decide in your favor, then **reward** him for that decision—*that* is mule wisdom.

Leading a Friend

Let's experiment with the set-up, wait, and reward method in leading. Before you try it out on your mule, find an unsuspecting friend who is willing to play a little game. Blindfold the friend so he will not react to your facial expressions. Wrap a belt around his wrist and back through the buckle. Let him be your resistant mule. You are going to have him try to figure out what you want. No other verbal instruction is allowed. Once commenced, no words are permitted from either party. You take the other end of the belt and pull steadily. Without words, keep up your patient pull until the friend reacts by movement. Release. You may find that the natural inclination of humans and mules is to resist the pressure and pull back. This is a natural instinct that you need to work through with your mule.

First, you will reward with a release for any response. Once you get movement, you can then direct that energy in moving towards you. Pull steadily on the belt again until the friend actually prepares to take a step towards you. Release at the moment that you can visually see his attempt to move forward. Still with no words, try again until you get forward movement. Soon, you will quietly be leading your friend around the barnyard and will be ready to test this set-up, wait, and reward method on your mule. If the friend can't figure out what you want, you then will need to take some additional time to perfect your skills before approaching your mule.

Leading Is Not Just Following

Following is when the mule willingly follows behind you, as he does with other equines in the field. On the other hand, leading is when the mule walks with you even when he doesn't really want to. Here is a terrific way to get that mule to lead, not just follow. This is most effective in those early years when the mule foal first begins resisting, and it also works well for older mules.

Let's say your mule balks when leading. You want him to move forward. Think first if there is a mule-logical reason for him balking. Is there a dangerous or scary thing ahead? Okay, you have determined that he is not in any danger but is determined to stay put. Now think simply. Right now you have no movement, just a solid mass of defiance! Your mule has planted his feet and won't move. Instead of your immediate goal being to get your mule to walk forward willingly, you may need to lower your expectations and decide that what you want is for your mule to take one step forward only. Then you can rest for a minute. After the rest, you can ask for a second step and a rest—then another, and another. And pretty soon, your mule is willingly walking forward again.

Sounds good. "Hmm, how can I get this mule to take that first step forward?" you ponder. Well, think of what happens when you pull on his halter rope. Is there not pressure on the head of the mule that is uncomfortable for him? If you are standing still with pressure on your head in the same way, you would want to get rid of the pressure, right? So does the mule. Whatever movement it takes to ease the pressure on the head is most likely what the mule will eventually decide on doing. Now, which direction do you want your mule to move—back or to the side? No, you would like for him to take a step forward. If you stood in front of him and pulled on his halter/head, that may just be the right pressure on his head to cause the mule to question his current behavior of standing still. He may want to relieve the pressure by giving in to it and moving forward toward you. You then have one forward step! Success!

Okay, this is a good plan. Now to try it out. Take your stance in front of your mule and pull steadily on the halter rope (1—trying to get him to question his current decision). The mule surprises you by backing up! Don't give up; this behavior isn't so bad. What we had was no movement a moment ago. Now we have movement, it just isn't in the direction we want. That is okay. The toughest part with a balking mule is getting movement in the first place. We can always focus and direct his energy later to moving in the specific direction we want.

Do not punish him if he explores other options, and don't encourage him to choose in your favor with treats. Simply allow your mule the valued opportunity to decide for himself. He will appreciate the learning and remember it longer if it is his decision.

All right, at least we know that your mule is uncomfortable with the pulling and is trying to relieve that pressure. If backing up, moving the head around, or moving sideways (2—exploring other options) will relieve the pressure, then your mule will do just that. If moving forward will ease the pressure, this is what your smart mule will choose to do. What you need to do now is not to let the pressure off when he does back up or otherwise not move forward. Plant yourself so the harder he pulls, the more pressure he has on his head. If he is beginning to pull you away, just go with him reluctantly. He will stop when he realizes that he isn't getting what he wants, which is relief from the head pressure.

Some mules have a grand tolerance for backing up, as it has got them what they wanted in the past so many times. *Or*, they have a tendency to get scared at this pull and attempt to run away. Do not get so determined to hang onto the rope if your mule insists on running away. It is of vital importance that you do not let yourself get hurt by being dragged around the field. It may be that the next step is to consult a professional trainer. This

Photo courtesy of Kevin Bassett, K & L Farms, Texarkana, AR. Photo of Laura Bassett on Josie.

Mules are very wise. Make sure to weigh your mule's vote on those trail ride decisions.

problem can be a lack of thorough training. We know it's important to correct these problems when they first begin, but sometimes that moment in time has already passed. To overcome recurring problems such as these, professional assistance may be required.

If your mule insists on backing up, you must lower your expectations from formerly wanting your mule to walk forward willingly, to wanting him to take one step forward, to wanting your mule to stop backing up. You really have to be flexible in your training and only attempt a goal that is the very next step from where your mule is right this second.

Now, the mule has either simply stopped backing or has backed into something unpleasant, which I hope you have allowed (one more way a mule trains himself!). Upon the stopping, release the pressure to reward him for stopping. Hurrah, you have success!

Stay right where you both are, get in front of him, and pull on that halter rope again. This time, your resistant mule moves his body sideways. Keep up the firm stance and go with him if necessary (unless he is determined to run away). Again, let go and release the pressure as soon as he stops moving around. Soon, you will stand in front of him and pull on the halter rope and he will think about taking a step forward (3—decide upon the path of least resistance).

Before the mule takes that step, he has to *think about* taking that step. It is beneficial to recognize his behavior when a mule is thinking about doing what you want him to do, and then reward him for that thought. As you would reward for the actual step, rewarding for the thought of the step is what precedes the step. This behavior can be as basic as perking the ears forward, lowering his head to scope out what is before him, or shifting his body weight to prepare to lift the leg for a step.

TRAINING HAS TO BE THOROUGH FROM THE START. THERE IS NOTHING WORSE THAN A HALF-TRAINED MULE.

So here you are, pulling on the head of your mule, and he shifts his weight, preparing to move forward. Immediately release and praise him wondrously! Give him a moment's rest to digest what just happened before you ask for another forward motion. Pull again, and watch him shift his weight again and maybe lower his head to look at what is in front of him. Again, release and praise for the thought of moving forward. Rest. In another minute, ask for forward movement again. Rather than just shifting weight, this time keep the head pressure a mite longer, until the weight shifting is coupled with a picking up of the leg, or until he does the next smallest order in this process (4—does it). Hurrah! Success, again! He has decided in your favor!

With the first step, your smart mule is experimenting to see if this action will take the pressure off his head—which is his goal. You must immediately release the hold on his halter and praise him wondrously for choosing this option! The instant that mule moves forward, you must release your hold or the whole system is null and void. He is trying to escape pressure and you want that to happen, so for goodness sake reward him the instant he decides to go your way.

Realize that you have succeeded tremendously if he only takes one step forward. Don't expect the moon; just settle for what he decides to give you and build on that. Do the same procedure a moment later for two steps and you will find that it takes him much less time to explore and decide upon the forward motion as long as he has been rewarded in a timely manner and sufficiently. You want the mule to think, "Hmm, moving forward eased the pressure last time, will it work this time?" It is up to you to make sure it will work for your mule every time. Reward each time the mule makes the effort to move forward. Pretty soon this smart mule will be leading in all circumstances, not just mindlessly following the leader.

This is what training is all about. When the mule feels pressure, he needs to learn to give in to that pressure, not resist it as is his natural inclination. If he were tied to a tree and he was pulling against the tree, he would eventually decide to move forward to stop the pressure on his head when he realized pulling back was creating more pressure and it wasn't getting him what he wanted.

If you pull and release before you get any forward movement or thought, your mule will not do anything but stand there. What reason does he have for questioning his original decision of balking? In the mule's mind, the pressure is already off at times (when you release), so all he has to do is outwait you until you release. Some handlers have a tendency to pull and release when they are vocally encouraging their mule to do what they want. [Pull] "Oh, come on now [release], [pull] I know you can do it" [release]. The best way to learn this method of set up, wait, and reward is to turn off your vocal cords!

Sometimes a mule gains wonderful progress after given time to think about it. If you are working on something specific with your mule and you aren't sure if you have accomplished anything, don't despair. It is just fine to leave on a good note and forget about the lesson for the day. Go back the next day and try it again. If you've been on the right track, your mule may have gotten it in his rest time and may now perform much more willingly.

Game-Playing in Bridling

The mule can easily become an extension of the owner's personality. Just as children will test you to your maximum, so will a mule. And when he finds your weak spot, he will milk it to the end! Mule games are so much fun to play it is difficult to convince both the mule and the handler to stop. Remember, it takes two to play the games, and if one party is enticing the other, even on a subconscious level, the games will probably persist.

Photo courtesy of Carole Showers, Bakersville, NC. Photo of Chuck Showers and Kate.

Listen to what your mule is saying. Only then can you make the best decision on your plan of action. Kate and Chuck are speaking volumes.

Here is an example of mule game-playing. You have taught your mule to wear a bridle. It seems that he has learned pretty well until one day you attempt to bridle him and all of a sudden he refuses to let you touch his ears (when there was no previous concern with the ears) and he throws his head up and away from you. First, realize that there may be a mule-logical reason your mule doesn't want to be bridled. Are you rubbing the headstall on an eye when you are bridling? Are the training sessions causing him undue stress? If all is well, then he may be playing games with you.

If you take the bridle away and hit or yell at him, he has just won. The reason the mule is throwing his head is to get you to take that bridle away. He will endure the yelling and anger since they are minor problems to contend with, especially if in the end he gets what he wants, which is to stop you from bridling him and therefore working him.

If you then try again and the same result occurs (as it probably will), he'll magnify his response and throw his head even further. If you respond more aggressively, your mule is happy since he has gotten one up on his owner by creating anger, which in a mule's mind means he has won the game! The key is to keep your cool and continue with the bridling even when the mule decides he is going to have a problem with it. It is essential that you take the time and patience that you need right then—when the problem starts—before it becomes a habit. He will quickly learn that you won't give in to his games, and he will come around to being bridled, easily.

If allowed to win (you get mad, give up, or otherwise don't continue the process calmly and determinedly until you can leave on a good note), the mule takes this event result in for future reference and may continually play this and other games. He gets so much enjoyment out of winning over his handler that he constantly attempts game-playing. A rule of thumb: if you allow the mule to win his first game, you will have many more to contend with. If you can clearly see that this episode will continue without your winning, it may be necessary to lower your expectations. Instead of bridling him, leave on a good note by having him remain calm while you rub his ears with your hands or rub the bridle over his ears without actually putting it on. Given time to think about it, the mule may very well decide to accept the bridle when you return. This takes reading your mule accurately and weighing it against your own ability, experience, and patience.

Photo courtesy of Michelle Dirkse, Seattle, WA.

If you are smarter than your mule, this scene will be an occasional
occurrence instead of a daily ritual.

Catch That Mule!

Again, it is important for the handler to realize that in all game-playing,
there is a choice made by both the handler and the mule to play the game.
By no means is it the "fault" of the mule when the handler finds himself in
the throes of mule games.

Quite often you will find a handler, halter in hand, in the middle of a field,
burning mad, because the mule he is trying to catch is running in the
opposite direction! Take a look at that mule; more than likely, he is having
a ball out there defying his handler. He has just proven once again that he
can outwit his human companion!

If the handler simply decided not to play, he then would figure out what it
took to catch his mule. It seems that it's easier to get caught up in the games
and lose than it is to use your brain to figure out what it will take to catch
your mule. No, I'm not talking about bribing with food or roping him.

First, take a look at why your mule does not want to be caught. Does he not
want to be around you? Maybe the mule is afraid of you. And maybe for
good reason, if each time you work him it ends in a battle or is unpleasant
for him. Make catching him pleasant and something he wants to do. How
about simply spending some time in the field with him just scratching,

petting, brushing, or talking to him? Food does make a good bribe, but use it only occasionally.

Are you feeding him food that is too hot for the amount of work asked of him and therefore he has an overabundance of energy? If he is in a very small pasture or a box stall and you have turned him out in a large pasture, maybe he doesn't want to go back to the stall. Maybe his natural energy is too much for the limited expression that comes with living in a stall. Maybe you are trying to put him away too soon and he needs to get more energy out.

If your young mule seems to be afraid of you, squat down below his eye level where you are not quite so threatening, and allow him to come to you and smell you. Do not try to reach up and grab him, or you will frighten him even more and he may never again try to come close enough to smell you. You can offer your hand for him to smell, and if he is close enough to you, a simple scratch on the chest or neck is a good step towards winning trust. It is important to remember that your mule wants to have a relationship with you. Allow him to do so at his own pace if you have a distrustful and reluctant mule to bring around.

Figure out a routine where you know you can catch your mule. Sometimes if the big field has a good corner, a barn, or a smaller pen attached, you can herd the mule into this area *away from his buddies.* The key is to find a place he wants to get out of and then block his outward path. If his buddies are outside the opening, your mule will try hard to go to them. If you are in his way, he will at least have his head towards you, going from side to side, to try and get around you. If he isn't focused on escaping, he would rather point his head in the corner and his rear towards you. This is not a good stance! So make sure you have action that you can direct in your desired manner. When he realizes he cannot get around you, let him settle, and then gently walk up to him, praising him for standing still. There should be some resignation in his eyes or a change in body language. If there isn't and he warily allows you to walk up to him, he just may bolt as you reach for him. If he resigns to you, his head will be down and he will be mostly calm. If he is still trying to win this game, his head will be up, his eyes will show mischief, and his body will be tense.

If you are in a corner of the field, this is more difficult, as there are more places your mule can get around you. If he does bolt around you, the key is to *stay in control*. Go as fast as you can and herd him back to the same corner where you can again be in control.

Each time you go to catch him, do not try to catch him in the big field, but herd him alone into this smaller area. If he just laughs at you and runs the other way, take control and keep him moving in the big field to get him to the smaller pen. Again, do not try to catch him anywhere but the smaller pen, and be certain he is alone. Soon, when he is tired of trying to dodge you (and failing, of course!), he will willingly go into the smaller area to be caught. When you both are learning this catching routine, make sure you have all day if that's what it takes, along with day-long patience. I would recommend catching him just to pet, touch, and brush him. Then let him go back to the big field. Make it desirable for your mule to be caught.

Soon, it will take minimal time to catch that "crazy mule." And, if you have played your cards right, it won't be long until he will want to be caught because he likes the special attention that he gets from you. Remember, your mule knows very clearly what is behind your smiling face. If you are having difficulties catching your mule, look inside to see if anger, revenge, prejudice, or dislike is truly in your heart.

This catching technique is a win/win situation. In a win/lose situation, where you win and the mule loses, you are tempted to gloat about how powerful you are. Personally, in a win/lose outcome, I may feel I'm hot stuff when I win. However, I really don't want the mule to lose. That mule is to be my partner, not my servant. In a win/win outcome, I feel much connection and appreciation when the mule does what I want him to do willingly.

Water-Crossing Fear

What if your mule's hesitancy to cooperate is because he is afraid and he has yet to trust your requests? What if that darned old flight instinct has gotten in his way of your intended goal? What does it take to create a willing mule when fear—real or imagined—is felt by that mule? Let's take an example that involves fear resistance. Say you are riding your mule and you approach a creek. In nearing the creek, the mule perks up his ears, lowers his head to look, and just as you expect him to step into the water, he freezes. Your mule has not yet decided to accept your judgment that the

Photo courtesy of Jennifer MacNeill-Traylor, Gypsy Mare Studios, www.gypsymare.com.

Water crossings don't have to be traumatic. Desensitize your mule to new and scary things and you will have a great mount.

water is a safe place to put his hooves. He is highly independent and is more apt to use his own judgment that this water may contain "mule monsters."

You will find that forcing him certainly does not help to ease your mule's fear of the water. Getting mad, yelling, threatening, and/or hitting only makes him more afraid of the creek, angry at you, and less willing to work with you today and tomorrow. This definitely will throw a wrench in your developing trust and partnership.

Let's think like a mule so maybe we can understand why he has reacted with fear, and what we can do to create a willing mule. The mule may be thinking, "What if there's quicksand in this water and I drown?" "What if I step into this water and a mule monster grabs me?" or "Maybe I can jump over it, or better yet—go home." Mules are naturally cautious where they put their feet since they do not like to get into trouble spots and risk pain or danger. Remember, in his natural wild habitat, losing his footing and falling may mean death if he is being pursued by a predator.

Look first to see if your decision is a good one. What type of footing is in the water bottom? Could your mule lose his footing on slippery rocks or soft, sinkable mud? If all is well in the creek bottom, realize that for some possibly accurate reason your mule is not trusting your judgment. Look to yourself first for the answer:

- Do you really believe he will do it, or not? If you believe he will learn what you are teaching him, he will. If you believe he probably won't "get it," he probably won't. In essence, what you believe will happen will most likely happen.

- Make sure he is capable of navigating the obstacle without endangering himself.

- Give him direction—why not dismount and lead him through the water yourself? Make sure you are at one side of him so if he jumps over the creek he doesn't land on you. Or better yet, have him follow a horse or another mule across, as they will show him that it is safe.

- Allow him independence and *trust* that he can figure out specifically where to put his own feet. You may not have noticed a much safer crossing ten feet downstream.

- Expect him to try—and encourage him with patience.

- Tell him he is wonderful when he crosses!

This will get you far with a mule. He appreciates your respect of his fear and intelligence, and this builds trust between the both of you. There is a fine line between mule smarts, fear, and game-playing. You need to be able to read your own mule accurately, and only experience will allow you to do that.

The Fear Point—Clipping

When you want calmness from your mule when he is afraid, you must ask for small increments of the big picture. The toughest part of this process is to determine what those small increments are, and which increments come before others, to result in the desired big picture of performing the task in peace. Here is a method to determine those increments when fear is involved, to remove the fear and create a willing mule.

Let's say you want to use the clippers on your mule to trim up his mane and tail. Your spooky mule is *not* going to stand for that loud, vibrating monster and would rather leave the scene. Okay, you have a problem. You want him to stand for clipping, and he doesn't want to. Why? Because he can't identify—and therefore is afraid of—the sound of the clippers. In order for him to stand quietly and calmly with no restraint, he has to become desensitized to the sound, the vibration, and all the movements he will be experiencing during the act of clipping.

In detail, your mule needs to be desensitized to hearing that frightening noise above him, below him, between the ears, on both sides of his body, and behind him. He then has to get used to the cord dangling and touching him on his legs, rear, back, neck, head, or anywhere else. Next, he must learn to accept the feel of the clipper vibration in all the above locations, and also to stand quietly as you pull on the mane and tail—as

Photo courtesy of Shawna Brown, Sagebrush Miniatures, www.sagebrushminis.com.

Attitudes begin early in life! *You must take and keep the leader position.*

you will be doing all of this when clipping. In the end, this mule has to have no fear of the complete process and trust that you are not going to hurt him. It's the only way he will willingly stand quiet.

Okay, time to ask some questions. Where is his fear level in relation to all that clipping entails? At what point does he get nervous and begin to react to that nervousness, and where is he already desensitized to parts of this clipping process? Let's say he doesn't like any part of this entire clipping idea. Then you must take this step by step from the beginning.

"Hmm...where do I start? Well, can I get him used to the noise of the clippers without actually clipping him? Well, yes I can. If I'm not going to clip him, and all I want is to get him used to the noise, I can hold the clippers a short distance away from him and turn the power on. Yes, that is a good start."

I tie him up, stand back, and turn on the clippers. Say the mule's eyes get wide and his head raises up. Maybe he even moves away from that fearful clipper sound. If he does this, then this is too close for his comfort and he is already afraid. The point where the mule begins to react in discomfort of the clippers is called his fear point. Let me take the clippers farther away. Now I'm ten feet away from him and I turn on the clippers. The mule focuses his ears curiously to this sound, but his head doesn't go up much and his eyes don't bug out. He is much more comfortable now when that scary monster is at this distance. Great—we have success. We have learned that from ten feet away, the mule has no fear.

If the mule is fine with the running clippers being in front of him at ten feet away, making that unnatural noise, but gets worried if you take them over to his right side, just bring the clippers back to the front again, where there is no fear. Then move them again to the right side. Soon he will have no concern with the ten-feet distance of the clippers at his right side. Now, put the clippers up over his head, to his left and right side, down near the ground, behind and all around him at the ten-feet distance. If he is not okay with it at any point, take the running clippers back to ten feet away (or as far as necessary beyond the fear point, until he stops reacting) and move them all around at that distance again. If you hit his fear point and he begins to react (swishing his tail, eyes getting fearful, head going up), you may need to just back away a step or two at that particular sensitive spot. Then bring the clippers forward until he is desensitized to the sound on that area for the ten-feet distance.

Your goal is to slowly close up that gap until there is no discomfort in the mule in any aspect of the sound of the clippers, no matter how close the clippers are to him. That means that you take the ten-foot radius between the mule and clippers and slowly lessen that gap—moving forward that fear point. With reassurance to the mule, bring the running clippers nine feet above him, below him, on both sides of his body, and behind him. Then do the same with eight feet, then seven feet, and so on. At each increment, make sure your mule is fine with the distance in all locations.

Soon the clipper sound is not a problem anywhere, and you can hold the running clippers within an inch of his body. It's time to go to the next step and work with the cord. With the clippers *off,* simulate clipping the mane and tail to get the mule used to the cord that may touch his neck, head, legs, or rear. Again, find his fear point and work it until it is dissolved in the same manner as the running clipper distance.

If you are not successful in your mule remaining calm through any of this process, just know that you cannot skip over these steps. You must work your mule through his fear points in order to have that mule totally accept the clipping process.

Next, test out the running clipper distance again. If all is well, put the back of the running clippers on the mule and allow him to feel the vibration. Again, watch for reactions and back off if you reach his fear point. Your goal now is for him to be totally okay with the vibration all over his body.

Then mess with his mane and tail. Pull on it gently, rub these areas. At any point you can repeat parts of this process to be assured that you have diminished or eliminated any fear points associated with clipping. When there is no more fear, go to work clipping that calm and willing mule.

Irritation is different than fear. *Know your mule.* An irritated mule is not the same as a fearful mule. Take it gentle and easy on the fearful mule; be firm and decisive with the irritated mule.

The Kicking Mule

There comes a time in a young mule's life where he may wish to assert his authority over humans in an attempt to establish who is where in the pecking order. This is natural; all equines must find out where they are in the line-up—who is above them, and who is below them. Also, your mule may need to establish or protect his boundaries. Either or both of these tasks can be done with the aid of his hind feet. Also, from the donkey side, the mule knows kicking will protect him if he is irritated, unsure, and fearful of what is around him.

There is a great technique to resolve mule kicking problems. This, as with all training techniques, is easiest and more completely accomplished when your kicking mule is young. For both horses and donkeys—and therefore, for mules—instinct is telling them feet are for traveling, for escaping danger, and not for humans to examine. If these critters allowed another to take their feet off the ground, they could lose balance and fall—which can mean death to them. Since humans are predators and equines are prey, it is easy to conclude that a human picking up a mule foot can arouse his fear of death.

Brushing—A Prelude to a No-Kick Mule

In an attempt to explain this technique for creating a no-kick mule, one must begin this process wherever the mule is most comfortable. Let's first think about what you want to accomplish in the big picture, and then break it down step by step.

You want to be able to get close to your mule, you want to be able to rub him all over, even on the rump, and you definitely want to feel comfortable running your hand down all his four legs. Once you do that, your goal is to have this mule willingly lift up his foot for you, nicely and calmly, with no concern, fear, or fight. Then you want to be able to move the foot around, extend it out, clean out the hoof, and mess with it in whatever way you choose—simulating farrier work.

All right, you know what you want. Of all these things, what can you do successfully right now? "Well, he doesn't mind me getting close to him. I can brush his body without him being too concerned about that." Great, you have a starting point. Ideally, you want to be able to brush the front legs with your mule being free to leave and not restrained in any way. Initially, your mule may need to be tied if he has never had his front legs handled in this manner.

Your goal is to be able to rub or touch your mule wherever you want, with him remaining calm and unconcerned. Use your soft brush and begin where he is comfortable. Brush in this order: neck, back, shoulders, down his front legs, rump, then down his hind legs. Stop when and where your mule shows concern, and work on that fear point before progressing to the other areas. If he becomes agitated when you brush his front legs, start there. Go back to where he is comfortable and work your way towards his fear point, the place he gets uncomfortable or agitated. If it is his lower legs that agitate him— remember, he may be sensitive there, as this is where an equine predator attacks in an attempt to disable him—go back to the shoulder and slowly work down again. Ease into the fear point until it is dissolved and a new fear point arises. Say, the knee is now okay, so you can work from the knee down. If he acts agitated, go back to where he is comfortable—the knee, the shoulder, or the back—and brush him there. Now again work your way below the knee until he stands quietly, with no concern.

Don't let his irritation affect you and bring out *your* fear. That is, don't yell at him to stand and don't demand anything from him. Just calmly move back to a comfortable spot for him. When he is settled, again brush into the uncomfortable spot. Pretty soon you will be brushing all up and down either front leg with your mule calm and relaxed.

Be careful—forcing him through his fear point when he is tied and unable to move away from you can be dangerous. If you are not aware of mule irritation signals, you may miss his nonverbal complaining. Most all mules will tell you there is a problem before they begin to kick. Sometimes severe actions such as kicking at a human is accumulated frustration from the mule attempting to tell you, but not getting through to you, that there is a problem. Be sure to be sensitive to other mule signals (swishing of the tail, stepping away, laying ears back, faking a bite) before a problem escalates. Acknowledge his signals by complying. Let him move around and be concerned without your reaction. Simply go back to an area that is not at his fear point until he settles down.

When you are successful in brushing his front legs calmly, then use your hand and rub the same area. If this is a problem, integrate the hand with the brush. Have the brush in one hand and brush down his front leg. Follow the brush with a stroke of your hand. When that is okay with him, then take the brush away and just use your hand. Run it down the leg; don't try and pick up the foot at this point. When your mule is completely comfortable with you messing with his lower front leg, only then can you think about picking it up off the ground.

Now, this whole process may take weeks if you have an older, fearful mule. This process may take minutes if you don't.

Every once in a while, you will find a mule that is fine with you touching his leg but simply will not let you lift his front foot. Or, your mule will never let you touch his cannon bone area. Note that it is possible that your mule may be in pain. If the touch on the front legs is way too difficult than anything else you have done with him, he may have a leg injury that never healed properly. Or, lifting his front leg may be irritating a back problem. And as much as your mule wants to comply, he wants even more to stay as far away from pain as possible. If you suspect injury or pain, seek professional help. (I mean for the mule, but it might not hurt the human either!)

Once you get the front legs handled calmly without incident, only then can you think about the hind legs. This is a technique to let him kick to his heart's content without punishment, until he realizes kicking doesn't get him what he wants, which is to rid himself of the person and the process. When he realizes he is not getting what he wants, he will *decide* to stop kicking on his own. You will have allowed him the vital opportunity to teach himself to not kick (see "Forbidden Fruit" in this chapter).

Picking Up That Foot Safely

Again, make sure you have tied your mule so he can't leave town. Make sure you can brush him up high on his inner hind legs. If you can't do this safely, then brush his rear, and work your way to the inner hind legs. When you are able to comfortably put your brush inside his upper legs, do the same with your hand. The goal here is to be able to take a non-burning cotton lead rope—or equivalent—and feed it between his upper legs to grab it on the other side. So, prepare your mule by handling the upper and inner

Photo courtesy of Michelle Dirkse, Seattle, WA.

1: In picking up the leg with a lead rope, expect him to do some kicking. Be sure to position yourself out of the line of fire of that hoof!

hind legs, all the way around to his tail. When this is comfortable for him, take that lead rope and rub his inner hind legs with it. Take the end snap of the lead and feed it through his upper, inner hind leg and out under his tail. Hook the snap to a loose ring on the rope, or if the snap and rope are appropriate size, you can feed the smaller rope through the snap.

Keeping the looped lead high up on the leg, wiggle it around until you have the lead circling his upper thigh. Now loosen it by wiggling a bit, and drop it down to his lower rear leg. Now you have the lead around his rear leg just below the heel or above the coronet band. Tighten or snug it up quickly, as the feel of the rope can cause your mule to kick. If the lead isn't snug, he can kick it off and you are then back to square one. Give him a minute to relax. If he just gets tense and lifts his head, you are doing fine. If he moves around and gets scared, just go with him, making sure his movement doesn't dislodge the lead rope.

All right, your mule has stopped moving and is now a bit tense, wondering what you're going to do. Realize he is scared, not playing games, and treat him accordingly. Reassure your mule that you are not going to hurt him. Stand near his front feet or head (away from his rear, since he may be doing

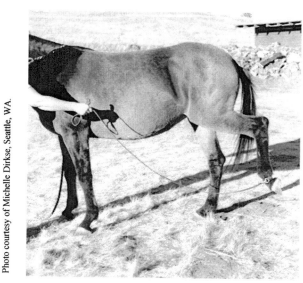

Photo courtesy of Michelle Dirkse, Seattle, WA.

2: There will be a moment when he stops kicking. Immediately let loose the pressure to show him that's what you want, and, as a reward.

some wild kicking and we know mules can kick out to the side, unlike a horse). Put some pressure on the lead attached to his hind foot. Watch him shift his weight to lift that leg. Again, work each step with your mule repeatedly until he is totally okay with what you are doing, illustrating no fear.

Now, put enough pressure on the lead where he will lift his foot. Watch out—here is where the kicking will come in (see illustration 1). Your goal right now is to just barely lift the foot and quickly put it down on the ground again. Later you can work on holding it up, but not right now. So, apply pressure to the lead rope until your mule shifts his weight, and as soon as he lifts his foot, take the pressure off and praise him. Keep the lead snug, as you don't want it to drop off the foot. You do want him to be able to put his foot down on his own power to ease his fears of standing on three legs.

Keep a tight grip—gloves work well—on the lead rope, and lift his foot again. If he so desires, allow your mule to kick to his heart's content. Go with him if he moves around. Make sure you allow your mule to put his foot back on the ground when he wants to. This will assure him that he still has control over his legs when he needs it. He may unbalance himself by

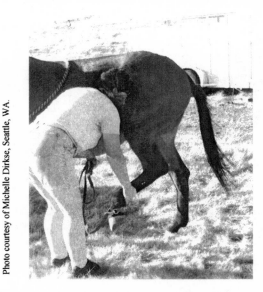

Photo courtesy of Michelle Dirkse, Seattle, WA.

3: Only after he totally relaxes into the lead, should you attempt to hold the leg with your hand.

kicking, which can frighten him. It is okay; just let him have his foot on the ground when he wants. If you hold the foot up when he needs to put it down, he will usually get more violent. This is his instinctual fear of death arising. You are trying to build trust in him. What you want is to show him he can lift his foot up when asked and put it down without losing balance and control and without anyone threatening or hurting him. Give him this time consideration and don't expect perfection from the start. Usually he will kick, kick, kick, down. When he puts his foot down, let off the pressure and praise him. He won't have a clue as to why you are praising him, but he soon will.

Pick up the foot again (set up). Allow kicking (wait) until he puts it down. Let the pressure off and praise him (reward). Once you are able to pull on the lead around the hoof, and your mule picks up his foot and does not kick, you are on the road to success. But you haven't arrived yet, so don't quit now!

As stated, the big-picture goal that we want to accomplish is to pick up the mule's hind foot with our hand, move it all around, pound on it as a farrier may do, and put it down at our choosing, with the mule so calm he is nearly falling asleep. Let's look at what we have so far, which is the mule picking up his foot when requested, and holding it tightly, not kicking at this moment. Our next step now is to have him relax into it a bit more.

Pick up his foot with the lead rope again and hold it a second or two, even when he wants to put it down. There is a fine line between instinctual fear of losing his balance, falling, and subsequent death *and* "If I fight and put myself off balance, I can have my foot down." This is hard to distinguish for the novice. Young mules in new situations usually don't have much game-playing in them, and those thoughts can be squelched easily if not given the circumstances to blossom.

Just know that if you hold his foot up and that fear of death arises, he will fight you like crazy—and there goes your and his trust factor! If you hold the foot up and he is game-playing, he will quit it fairly quickly when he learns you won't play. This depends upon how old your mule is and how long he has played this game. Keep up this process until your mule picks up his foot with a pull on the lead and relaxes his leg—making the lead heavier—instead of holding his leg tight, ready for kicks (see illustration 2). You then can move the leg around with the lead rope, out to the side, in under his belly, and out back. Careful—the latter promotes kicking, which can easily dislodge the lead rope.

When this is fine with your mule—we may be talking days or minutes—then you can pick up the foot with the lead and get close enough to touch it with your hand. Begin to substitute your hand with the lead rope—your mule should be calm for this process. Rub your hand up and down his relaxed leg. Take the weight off the lead rope and rest his leg on your hand (see illustration 3.). Move the leg around minimally with your hand. Go back to the lead rope and let his leg down. Do this several times, until this is not a lick of a problem with your mule. Keep the lead taut in your hand, run your other hand down his leg, and pick up the foot with your hand. Move it around and put it down again—yeah, success!! If the mule is totally calm, next you can do this without the lead rope at all!

The Forbidden Fruit—Wandering and Bucking

Have you ever fought and fought with your mule about something simple that he wanted to do, but you didn't want him to do it? Sometimes it is up to you to think a bit differently with your mule than is normal, to get the best

Photo courtesy of Michael E. Abrams, Florida A&M University, Tallahassee, FL, www.flwildflowers.com.

Stubborn? No, just resisting cooperation. Make sure your mule isn't resisting you for a mule-logical reason.

out of him. If your mule really wants to do something that you don't want, a human's normal thought is to stop him, prevent him, forbid him from doing it. Does this work? Well, sometimes for a short while, but usually not for long-term.

What works every time and for life? Consider giving him what he wants fully until he doesn't want it anymore. (Do not apply this to food consumption.) And when he no longer wants this "thing," he will forget about it and go on to something else. If his desire is forbidden fruit— meaning, you won't allow him to do it—this desire will linger or grow; rarely does it go away.

The other side of this coin is to ask yourself why you don't want him to do it. Quite often it comes down simply to human fear. Maybe you are afraid of getting hurt, of not being in control, or of him taking advantage of you. Look at what he wants to do and see if it really is so bad that you need to forbid him not to do it, or is it just triggering a fear that you do not want to feel?

For example, one day I was trail riding and this molly really wanted to wander off the trail and into the brush. I kept turning her back onto the trail. It began to irritate me that I had to constantly fight her and keep directing this mule back on the trail. I looked inside myself and found out that I just wanted to be the one in control, and she was fighting that aspect. Once I backed off of my focused desire to control, I looked at what she wanted to do. "Oh, that's not so bad," I thought, and then let her wander wherever she wanted. There were horses up ahead, so I knew that she wouldn't get very far away from them. This mule went up the hill, back down the hill, all around, through the brush and trees, and finally ended up back on the same trail, trotting to catch up with the horses. This curbed her desire to wander. She found out that it was harder work to walk through the brush, go uphill or downhill, and dodge the trees. And now that I wasn't trying to control her every move, it wasn't nearly as much fun to fight me. Besides, the horses ahead kept getting farther away! After that, she stayed on the trail on her own decision.

GIVE HIM WHAT HE WANTS UNTIL
HE DOESN'T WANT IT ANYMORE

Here is another forbidden fruit example. Say you put the saddle on your mule's back for the very first time. He is on a lunge line and really wants to get that saddle off his back. You keep jerking him back whenever he attempts to dislodge that nasty thing on his back, never allowing him to buck. Why do you not allow him to buck? Maybe it is because of your own fear of getting hurt: "If he bucks once, he will always be a bucker, and I may get thrown off if I'm in the saddle."

Training procedure continues, but in the mind of the mule, he still really wants to buck that saddle off as it is uncomfortable, has strange sounds, and flaps funny. One day, later down the road, you mount this mule for the first time. Without the lunge rope, he finally has the freedom to try and get that saddle off his back. So he begins this episode of bucking. Buck, buck, buck, and whoops, off goes you, the rider. "Hmm, this is interesting," he thinks. "Maybe more bucking will get rid of the saddle, too." And off he goes, rodeoing around the ring.

This episode is an extension of his former repressed desire to get the saddle off because of its funny sounds and feel. Your initial fear of getting hurt if he bucked caused you to not let him buck. And the result was that he bucked you off. So, your fear of getting hurt got you hurt. And on top of all that, he also learned that bucking will get the rider off if he ever needs this juicy tidbit of information.

Why not give him the opportunity to learn right up front to really accept the saddle? To produce the best and safest mule, give him what he wants until he doesn't want it anymore. Make sure his saddle is situated properly on his back and tight enough to stay on, even in the midst of a bucking rodeo. Also, make sure the saddle is an older, inexpensive one, so if he decides to roll (this is attempting to remove the saddle from his back, too), you won't lose your cool and try to stop him. Now, get out of the ring as quickly as you can! Allow him full opportunity to buck or roll to his heart's content.

It is a satisfying feeling for me to see an unbroken mule buck or roll, as there is considerably less chance that he will do this when I mount up. If he does not buck with the saddle, that is when I get worried about my safety as a rider! Allow him to buck or roll until he doesn't want to anymore. Then try to get him to buck. Get in the ring and move him around to see if movement irritates him enough to try and buck off the saddle. What you want is to be able to move him at any speed and for him to have no fear or concern of the saddle, accepting it as part of him.

Also, if you find a mule that bucks people off, this is the first place to start. Put that saddle on, get out of the ring, and watch him closely. His behavior will tell you whether he has a problem with the saddle or a problem with the rider. If he acts irritated with the saddle, bucks, or rolls, he probably never initially wanted to get rid of the rider, he simply wanted to get rid of the saddle. If he has absolutely no problem with the saddle and has forgotten it is on his back, then most likely he has a problem with a rider.

I have done my best to explain these techniques to you on paper. They still may be a bit confusing. Go out, work with your mule, and you will gain more information. Reread the section you are working on, go out, and practice some more. Soon it will all make sense.

There are so many possibilities of problems with mules, as with any other trained animal, that one cannot address them all. If I have done my job correctly, you now have a base of mule wisdom to tackle all forthcoming problems in the most effective manner. The ultimate goal is to create a willing partnership with your lifelong, long-eared partner.

CLOSING

In closing, I would like to express my appreciation to you for caring enough about mules to read this book. Please let your affection for mules, horses, donkeys, and all animals spill over to taking great care of them physically, mentally, emotionally, and spiritually. Humans have domesticated animals for our personal benefit and pleasure. It is up to us to provide excellent care, training, discipline, variety, and an abundance of love so they can live a full, happy, and healthy life, just as we humans strive to do for ourselves.

Cynthia Attar

INDEX

Infection, 113
Intense colors, 49, 50, 55
Israel, 8

Jack mules, 30, 44, 45
Jail, 108
Jumping, 19

Kind eye, 76
King Charles III, 10
King of Spain, 10
Koppertox, 111

Lifespan, 117
Lyons, John & Josh, 4

Maltese cross, 50
Marquis de Lafayette, 10
Memory, 93, 133, 146
Mount Vernon, 10
Mysia, 8

Norton, Virl, 21

October 26, 10, 24

Pack Scramble, 19
Packing, 19, 26, 64, 85, 98, 110, 133
Parelli, Pat, 4
Philosophy, 2, 134, 148
Plowing, 20
Pulling, 11, 18, 20, 24, 69, 75, 98, 129, 147, 153, 154, 155

Racing, 20, 21, 26, 69
Reining, 18

Riley, Harvey, 65
Roads, Michael, 5
Roberts, Monty, 4
Roping, 18, 26, 62, 158
Royal Gift, 10

Saddle, 10, 17, 31, 34, 60, 85, 91, 101, 132, 174, 175
Sally the Wonder Mule, 5, 6, 22, 44, 45, 104, 105, 106, 115, 124, 130, 131
Season. *See* Heat cycles
Self colors, 49, 50, 55
Set up, wait, and reward, 148, 149, 151, 156
Shedding, 109
Silvester, Bill and Oneta, 46
Smith, Penelope, 5
Sponenberg, Phillip, 49, 182
Spontaneous resistance of cooperation, 130
Sterile, 17, 29, 30, 36, 38, 40, 46
Stubborn, 67, 91, 100, 124, 129, 147

Tellington-Jones, Linda, 5
The Knight of Malta, 10
Thrush, 111
Trust, 66, 70, 71, 72, 76, 77, 93, 109, 111, 132, 133, 160, 161, 162, 163, 170, 172
Twins, 47, 48

Washington, George, 9, 10, 24, 34
Western, 20, 21, 26, 90
White Lightning, 46

PHOTO & ILLUSTRATION INDEX

179

SUGGESTED READING

Ainslie, Tom, and Bonnie Ledbetter, *The Body Language of Horses*. New York: William Morrow (1980). Very good book connecting the horse's physical actions with their emotional meaning.

Boone, J. Allen, *Kinship With All Life*. New York: Harper and Row (1976). Excellent book in learning that humans *can* have two-way, non-verbal communication with animals.

Green, Ben K, *Horse Tradin'*. New York: Knopf (1978). Humorous short stories of Ben Green's early life in the 1900s as a horse trader. This book has mule teachings spattered throughout.

Green, Ben K, *Some More Horse Tradin'*. New York: Knopf (1986). More great stories and teachings, prior to becoming a veterinarian.

Green, Ben K, DVM. *The Color of Horses*. Flagstaff, AZ: Northland Press (1974). A complete five-year study by veterinarian Dr. Green on the horse hide. A thorough explanation and understanding of coat color.

Hiby, Lydia, and Bonnie S. Weintraub, *Conversations with Animals*. Troutdale, OR: New Sage Press (1998). Lydia is a top animal communicator who has helped many folks, including the author. This book is a recollection of conversations she's had with animals.

Miller, Robert M., DVM, *Imprint Training*. Colorado Springs, CO: The Western Horseman (1994). An excellent and thorough how-to book that teaches the techniques and impacts of imprinting a foal.

Myers, Arthur, *Communicating with Animals*. Chicago: Contemporary Books (1997). An informative book of interviews with various animal communicators in the country.

Patent, Dorothy Hinshaw, *Horses and Their Wild Relatives*. New York: Holiday House (1981). This book helps to separate the confusion on the types of zebras and today's wild asses.

Riley, Harvey, *The Mule*. New York: Dick and Fitzgerald (1867). Wonderful information about the mule as heavy work animals for the U.S. government, in the late 1800s.

Roads, Michael J, *Talking with Nature*. Tiburon, CA: Kramer (1987). Detailed experiences by the author in ESP-type of communication with animals, birds, plants, and other earth forms.

Shapiro, Robert, and Julie Rapkin, *Awakening to the Animal Kingdom*. San Rafael, CA: Cassandra Press (1988). Excellent channeled material of various animal spirits speaking in reference to humans.

Smith, Penelope, *Animal Talk: Interspecies Telepathic Communication*. Point Reyes Station, CA: Pegasus Publications (1982). A great how-to book for humans interested in developing telepathic communication with animals.

Sponenburg, Phillip, DVM, *Equine Color Genetics*. Ames, IA: Iowa State University Press, (1996). This book is inundated with all horse colors that exist today! A bit confusing, yet a good reference book on identifying horse colors and the variations.

Tellington-Jones, Linda, and Ursula Bruns, *An Introduction to the Tellington-Jones Equine Awareness Method*. New York: Breakthrough (1989). Valuable information and exercises that help to understand and modify the behaviors of horses.

Tellington-Jones, Linda, with Sybil Taylor, *The Tellington Touch*. New York: Viking Penguin Group (1992). Outstanding techniques for solving difficulties and problems in all animals using tried and true methods of touch.

Twelveponies, Mary, *There Are No Problem Horses, Only Problem Riders*. Boston: Houghton Mifflin (1982). Identifying horse problems in the rider!

REFERENCES

[1] Sigmund A. Lavine and Vincent Scuro, *Wonders of Mules*. New York: Dodd, Mead and Co., 1982.

[2] Peter Nalle, miner, in Bonne Terre, Missouri.

[3] John Randolph Spears, *Illustrated Sketches of Death Valley and Other Borax Deserts of the Pacific Coast*. Chicago and New York: Rand, McNally and Co., 1892, 99.

[4] Robert Ivan Miller, *Mules*. Small Farmers Journal 12, no. 3.

[5] Emerson Johnson, *The Mules of the Game*. The Country Gentleman Magazine.

[6] Peter Chew, *The Comeback of the Mule*. Smithsonian, November 1983.

[7] Hutchins, Paul, and Betsy Hutchins, *The Modern Mule*. Denton, TX: Hee Haw Book Service, 1981.

[8] Dick Spencer, *Probably More Than You Ever Wanted to Know About Mules*. Western Horseman Magazine 54, July 1987.

[9] Ed A. O. McKinnon and J. L., Voss, *Equine Reproduction*. Philadelphia: Lea and Febiger, 1993. Reprinted in The Brayer 29, no. 3.

[10] Elwyn Hartley Edwards, *Wild Horses: A Spirit Unbroken*. Stillwater, MN: Voyageur Press, 1995.

[11] Meridith Hodges, *Mule Crossing*. Mules Newsletter, August 1987.

[12] Ben K. Green, DVM, *The Color of Horses*. Flagstaff, AZ: Northland Press, 1974.

[13] Phillip Sponenburg and Bonnie V. Beaver, *Horse Colors*. New York: Breakthrough Publications, 1983.

[14] Ben K. Green, DVM, *The Color of Horses.* Flagstaff, AZ: Northland Press, 1974.

[15] Harvey Riley, *The Mule.* New York: Dick and Fitzgerald, 1867.

[16] T. Lee Rumbaugh, *Evolution of the Mule Saddle.* Mules Newsletter, May 1987.

[17] Betsy Hutchins, *Breeding for the Saddle Mule.* Western Horseman Magazine, December 1970.

[18] Robert Ivan Miller, *Mules.* Small Farmers Journal 12, no. 3.

[19] Harvey Riley, *The Mule.* New York: Dick and Fitzgerald, 1867.

[20] Jamie Jackson, *The Natural Horse.* Flagstaff, AZ: Northland Press, 1992.

[21] Ben K. Green, DVM, *Horse Tradin'.* New York: Alfred A. Knopf, 1978.